THE
DISTANCE
MANAGER

THE
DISTANCE
MANAGER

A Hands-On Guide to Managing Off-Site Employees and Virtual Teams

KIMBALL FISHER
MAREEN DUNCAN FISHER

McGraw-Hill

New York   San Francisco   Washington, D.C.   Auckland   Bogotá
Caracas   Lisbon   London   Madrid   Mexico City   Milan
Montreal   New Delhi   San Juan   Singapore
Sydney   Tokyo   Toronto

Library of Congress Catalog Control Number: 00-135242

McGraw-Hill

A Division of The **McGraw·Hill** Companies

14 15 16 17 18 19 20   DOC/DOC 1 5 4 3 2 1 0

ISBN 0-07-136065-4

This book was set in Janson Text by North Market Street Graphics.

Printed and bound by R. R. Donnelley & Sons Company.

How to Contact the Publisher
To order copies of this book in bulk, at a discount, call the McGraw-Hill Special Sales Department at 800-842-3075; or 212-904-5427.

To ask a question about the book, to contact the author, or to report a mistake in the text, write to Richard Narramore, Senior Editor, at richard_narramore@ mcgraw-hill.com.

To our teachers and mentors, especially Carl Axelsen, the late Gene Dalton, the late Bill Dyer, Kate Kirkham, Laree Mugler, Pat Murray, Horace Parker, Joyce Ricklefs, Bonner Ritchie, Jim Thompson, Paul Thompson, Alan Wilkins, and Warner Woodworth.

Contents

Introduction

Managing from a Distance

Any group of people who need each other to take effective action for the company can do so immediately without regard for organization or location.

Mark Armentrout, Manager of Information Technology
Arco Exploration and Production

Bruce Ellis, formerly a regional sales director for AT&T, worked in an office in Denver, Colorado. But the salespeople who reported to him didn't. They lived in Minneapolis, Las Vegas, Salt Lake City, San Francisco, and Los Angeles. They were "all over the map," he explains, "and sometimes their office was at the customer's location." Bruce was what we call a *distance manager:* someone charged to lead people who are not normally located together at the same place at the same time. Although this is not a new situation, many more managers than before now find themselves in the same circumstances as Bruce. In fact, the organizations where managers lead only people who work regularly together at the same time and place are becoming rare. Says Yong-In Shin, a manager with the I.T. organization in Intel Corporation: "In our part of the company, if you have more than 10 people reporting to you, you have to expect to have a virtual team with people who live in several different locations."

These leaders have special challenges associated with managing from afar. How can you ensure top performance from people you see only infrequently? How do you help people work together cohesively when they aren't "co-located" (the word experts use to describe people working at the same site)? How do you communicate effectively with people who work all over the map? How do you lead teams composed of people both inside and outside of your organization? How do you deal with the challenges of motivation and coaching from afar?

From our own personal experience we can tell you that in some ways being a distance manager is like trying to be a leader with your hands tied behind your back while you're wearing a paper bag over your head. You can't see, hear, or speak face-to-face with those you're supposed to be leading. And you're not close enough to lend them a hand. As owners of a consulting firm, we must often coordinate activities not only with our consultants in Portland, Boston, and Saint Louis, but also with affiliated independent consulting firms in places such as South Africa, Canada, and Australia. This is difficult work. While these virtual organizations can have unparalleled benefits that come from coordinating richly diverse experience and abilities, they also pose a tremendous managerial challenge.

What once were the dilemmas faced only by those at the top of large corporations are now common concerns. No longer an elite minority composed primarily of senior corporate executives, distance managers are found at every level of both private and public organizations.

Today's technologies and business requirements both allow and demand distance management like never before. If you are a leader, you can no longer avoid distance management—you can only choose to do it well or do it poorly. The distance managers who do it well will offer a tremendous competitive advantage to the operations they lead. Those who do not may watch the unraveling of both their organizations and their careers.

What Is in This Book?

We wrote this book to provide pragmatic advice on how to be a distance manager. It isn't easy. Some have argued that is isn't even possible to create an effective team when the members are geographically distributed. As Mark Armentrout, an information technology executive at Arco, explains, "You shouldn't use a virtual team unless you have to. It's much easier to use co-located teams. But sometimes you have no choice." Arco, for example, is currently building a production facility on one of the largest oil fields discovered in Alaska in the last 10 years. Key members of the construction team, however, are located all over the place. The engineering firm is located in Calgary, Alberta; construction resources are located both in Alaska and in Corpus Christi, Texas; and research is in Plano, Texas. All must work together seamlessly to ensure a successful project. This requires effective distance leadership.

We want to share with you what we have learned from the successful distance managers we have studied. They come from dozens of organizations ranging from *Fortune* 100 companies to new dot.com companies with only a handful of employees. These distance managers work in high-tech companies, petrochemical and forest products conglomerates, consulting firms, middle schools, consumer goods companies, e-business start-ups, telecommunications companies, and other operations. Many of them come from companies that are now household names like Hewlett-Packard, Sun Microsystems, Weyerhaeuser, Intel, Andersen Consulting, Dell Computers, Xerox, and Procter & Gamble, and others come from organizations (like WebSentric) that you might not have heard of. They are sales managers, project leaders, executives, management consultants, information technologists, and a host of others who share the common experience of being distance managers.

How Is This Book Organized?

The book is divided into four parts that cover the key principles, skills, techniques, and technical tools required to succeed as a distance manager (see Figure I.1, "The Four Sections of *The Distance Manager*"). In Part I, "Distance Managing: The Foundation Principles," we'll review the characteristics and skills required to be an effective distance leader. We'll discuss the 7 key competencies of effective distance leadership, 5

Part 1: Distance Managing: The Foundation Principles
The basic principles of distance management, including: competencies, effectiveness cripplers, employee expectations, and types of virtual teams

Part 2: Staying Connected and Coordinated: The Dos and Don'ts
The best practices of distance management, including: distance coaching, training, motivating, trust building, team building, performance management, and celebration

Part 3: The Distance Technology Handbook
Tips for using enabling technologies such as telephones, voice mail, teleconferencing, videoconferencing, e-mail, Webtools, Webconferencing, electronic whiteboards, shared files, and more

Part 4: The Distance Manager in Action
Examples of how real managers in Xerox, International Paper, Hewlett-Packard, and Weyerhaeuser overcome the challenges of distance leadership

---

Figure I.1   The Four Sections of *The Distance Manager*

things that can cripple your effectiveness, 10 expectations employees have of their distance leaders, and the 6 different types of virtual teams you may be called on to lead.

In Part II, "Staying Connected and Coordinated: The Dos and Don'ts," we will review the best practices of distance leadership, including things like coaching, training, motivating, team building, and celebrating from afar. We will also consider common dos and don'ts associated with building trust from a distance, helping employees who work at home, and the necessity of certain face-to-face activities.

Part III, "The Distance Technology Handbook," focuses on tips for using the technologies that enable distance management. We'll review how to set up a virtual office and pass along recommendations from successful distance leaders on how to use e-mail, intranets and extranets, teleconferencing, videoconferencing, electronic whiteboards, and a variety of Web tools.

In Part IV, "The Distance Manager in Action," we'll tell you the stories of four extraordinary operations in more detail. We'll look at a Xerox sales team, a team of middle-school consultants at Champion International, the distance product development practices at Hewlett-Packard, and a Weyerhaeuser business turnaround case. In this section you'll see how real distance managers have faced and overcome real-world problems. We'll review their challenges and pass along their tips for succeeding in this difficult but increasingly common work environment.

Book Topics and Tips

You'll find hundreds of tips and examples sprinkled throughout the book. Most of the tips will be highlighted and numbered in the chapters to ensure easier reference (as follows in our first tip for you to consider):

Tip number one: Not all of the tips in this book will be appropriate for your situation. We have tried to include tips with broad applicability. However, as you know, what works in one company won't necessarily work in yours. Apply only those tips that will be appropriate for the technologies, employees, and unique cultural requirements of your operation.

Chapter Order

Although chapters in each part may reference earlier chapters or introduce future ones, they are not written in a way that requires you to have read earlier chapters in order to understand later ones. You can follow the chapters in the order that satisfies your interests and needs.

We do, however, recommend that you review the foundation principles before you attempt to practice the technology tips. Our experience is that two distance leaders—one who has mastered the foundation principles, and one who has not—may apply the same tip with dramatically different results. The leader who masters the principles will do a number of extra things to ensure the proper use of distance learning and communication technologies—and thereby ensure a better result than the leader who focuses only on the selection of the proper hardware and software.

Good News and Bad News for the Distance Manager

The good news is that there are some things distance managers can do to more effectively deal with the communication, coordination, and coaching challenges highlighted in this introduction. These include the advanced use of e-mail, file sharing, the Internet, teleconferencing and videoconferencing, and other modern techniques and technologies that we will review in more detail in the book.

But the bad news is that technology alone is insufficient. For example, experienced distance managers won't be surprised to find that the leaders whose stories appear in this book confirm that there are certain things (like team start-ups, conflict resolution, and performance appraisals) that can only be done effectively face-to-face. This is bad news to experienced leaders, because they know that as difficult as it is to master technology (the so-called "hard stuff" of business), mastering interpersonal relationships (the so-called "soft stuff" of business) is even harder—especially from a distance.

More good news is that we have also learned that certain management techniques and paradigms work equally well whether the employees are on-site or off-site. Of course certain management techniques—particularly those associated with the authoritarian styles and practices of the Industrial Age—don't work. But many managers have come to believe that those practices may be obsolete even in operations with co-located staff anyway.

More bad news, however, is that while being a distance manager has its rewards, the skills involved are very difficult to master. Building trust from a distance and coaching from afar are especially problematic, so we have devoted full chapters to both of these skills.

Why Traditional Management Skills Don't Help the Distance Manager

Traditional management skills are often based on the assumption that the employees are located just down the hall; that they are all there at the same time; and that they share a common culture. One of the authors of this book, for example, was taught in a business school class that it was management's job to control the workforce. The distance leaders we interviewed, however, firmly suggested that their role is *not* to control, but rather to teach people in remote offices how to control themselves. The distance manager can't control from afar, if control means managing the day-to-day responsibilities of a widely distributed workforce. They aren't there enough to do that (and it probably isn't the best way to manage anyway).

It's Time for Distance Managers

As we will demonstrate in this book, there are a number of great histor-ical leaders who figured out how to master distance management. Some of them became masters before there were any good technology aids. Julius Caesar found ways to oversee a vast world empire without the conveniences of modern communication technologies. Alexander the Great, Napoleon Bonaparte, and Joan of Arc found ways to motivate, discipline, and coordinate vast armies. Paul, the Christian apostle, helped to lead the early church using epistles—letters written from afar.

These truly great leaders motivated and inspired in ways that spanned space, time, and culture. Some led so compellingly that their messages have survived over the greatest distance of all: from beyond their graves.

Summary

The sales, service, consulting, project, product development, e-commerce teams, and countless other operations driven by the realities of gobal business all have something in common: the challenges of coordinating people from a distance. This has tremendous implications for managers, who are now expected to lead people they seldom meet face-to-face. Many of the traditional skills and perspectives that aided the manager who led people located in a single building fall far short of meeting the need when those he or she is charged to motivate, coordinate, and develop are scattered across the city, country, or world. New manage-ment strategies and techniques are needed. In the next several chapters we'll review the key skills, paradigms, and practices of leading from afar that can make you a competent and confident distance leader.

Kimball Fisher
Mareen Duncan Fisher

Acknowledgments

W̶E WANT TO EXPRESS our sincere appreciation to our editor, Richard Narramore, for his many suggestions and remarkable insights. His foresight and commitment to seeing this book completed has been a source of great encouragement.

We also wish to extend heartfelt thanks to the many people who shared their experiences and knowledge with us. It has been an honor to learn from them and to have the opportunity to share their stories in this book. We are especially grateful to the entire Champion Middle School Partnership Lead Team: Jim Hoffman, Neila Connors, Judy Enright, Jim Forde, Jim Garvin, James Gautier, Howard Johnston, Jerry Lynch, and John Van Hoose. We have been inspired not only by their stories of successful virtual teaming, but by the goodness of the work they do. Their contribution to the betterment of education for generations to come is both exciting and inspirational.

Xerox Corporation, with its long and successful history with distance management, also deserves special gratitude for sharing vital learnings with us. And we would like to acknowledge the special contribution of Hewlett-Packard and Weyerhaeuser Company, from whom we have been learning for many years, as well.

Special thanks to the other individuals who spent so many hours helping us understand the realities of distance leadership, including: Mark Armentrout, Arco Exploration and Production; Bill Barhydt, WebSentric; Peter Bartlett, Hewlett-Packard; Bill Blankenship, Weyerhaeuser Company; Lynn Buchanan, Weyerhaeuser Company; Curt

Crosby, Sun Microsystems; Eric Ecklund, Xerox; Dion Eusepi, Hewlett-Packard; Jill Freeman, Weyerhaeuser Company; Steve Gibbons, Principal Financial Group; Mike Kuczwara, Procter & Gamble; Jerry Mannigel, Weyerhaeuser Company; Jay Mehta, Weyerhaeuser Company; Mark Nyman, MediaOne; Dee Oviatt, Pioneer Hi-Bred International, Inc.; Karen Petty, Capital One; J. Bonner Ritchie, Ph.D., Brigham Young University; Yong-In Shin, Intel; Richard Thier, Xerox; and Charlie Wagner, Altura Energy.

We also wish to thank our colleagues of the Social Technical Systems Roundtable for their reflections and comments that helped to refine our early thinking on many of these concepts. Likewise, the writings of leaders in the field of organization development have helped to formulate much of our thinking over the course of several years. In particular we acknowledge the remarkable influence of the late Eric Trist and Fred Emery. The legacy of workplace dignity crafted by these two great minds has been a source of inspiration to us throughout our careers. For this volume of work we have also drawn on the writings of Ed Lawler, Frederick Hertzberg, Ed Schein, Richard Walton, Marvin Weisbord, Jessica Lipnack, and Jeffrey Stamps.

We also wish to express appreciation to those who have allowed us to use copyrighted sources in this book. Special thanks to The Fisher Group, Inc. (*www.thefishergroup.com*) for allowing the use of numerous models and training tips. In particular, portions of their Leadership Skills program for leaders and managers, their Team Resource Skills program for those in staff and technical expert roles, and their Team Tools program have provided concepts and information that we have used throughout the book. Portions of Chapter 1 were adapted from our book *The Distributed Mind: Achieving High Performance Through the Collective Intelligence of Knowledge Work Teams* (AMACOM, New York, 1998) and from Kimball's book *Leading Self Directed Work Teams* (McGraw-Hill, revised edition, New York, 2000). They are used by permission of the authors.

Finally, this book could not have been completed without the help, support, and everyday teachings provided by our colleagues Stephanie Ford, Caroline Wethern, and Kelly Cziep. They are wise and patient teachers to these two perpetual students.

I

Distance Managing: The Foundation Principles

The Seven Competencies of an Effective Distance Manager

But of a good leader, who talks little,

When his work is done, his aim fulfilled,

They will all say, "We did this ourselves."

Lao-tzu

About 550 B.C.

DOUG LOEWE IS the European marketing manager for CompuServe, a half-billion-dollar Internet company. But he isn't located in London or Munich, where his sales and service teams are. He lives 5000 miles away, in New York City. With the aid of a network-capable laptop computer and a cell phone, he manages a workforce that lives on a different continent. He receives and responds to about 50 e-mails a day. That technology helps, but it's not enough to really lead his team. So, he travels frequently to spend real time with them. Rather than spending all of his time in management meetings when he is on the road, Loewe tries to get out to see customers with his sales and service team members. He plans his schedule three months in advance, so that salespeople can arrange to include him on sales calls. This face-to-face time is essential to provide appropriate coaching and offer real support to the field. But he has to use other methods and tools to supplement the personal interaction.[1]

How can Loewe manage from a distance? Not by traditional supervisory methods. He has neither the time nor the opportunity to direct the day-to-day tasks of a widely dispersed workforce like an on-site manager could. Nor does he think that's the best way to manage. His salespeople need to be self-supervising. "The system will fail if the team is made up of people who need constant prodding to get the work done," he says. The salespeople who don't fit in this arrangement are the ones who "aren't used to doing things that they're not told to do." They have to be self-starters, Loewe says. If you happen to be distance-managing people who aren't self-starters, you have a problem. (There are, however, coaching techniques that you can use to improve the performance of non-self-starters—even from a distance; we'll tell you how in Chapter 5, "The Distance Coach: Getting Peak Performance.")

If Loewe's role as a distance manager isn't to prod workers into action, what is it? One answer is to teach them how to work together to form a more effective team. For example, he tells the story of how one client with offices in London, England, Munich, Germany, and Cambridge, Massachusetts, was working with multiple salespeople from his company. But because each salesperson was trying to get the credit for closing the deal, they weren't sharing information with each other about the rapidly changing client situation. Account progress ground to a halt until Loewe had the salespeople talk to each other. When they realized why they needed to collaborate (*no one* gets credit for a sale that is never made), e-mails began to fly back and forth until the account surged forward and a number of deals were closed. "The salespeople must recognize the value of teamwork so they will do it on their own," he concludes.[2]

Effective distance leaders are competent leading from afar. They create communication networks to provide a virtual presence with those they lead and (as illustrated in this short example) to help team members find both the means and the motivation to hook up with each other as well. Distance leaders—like sales managers, product development managers, project leaders, executives, or anyone else who seldom sees those he or she is charged to lead—use their valuable face-to-face time with others for the highest-leverage activities. Not the least of these activities is teaching others how to manage themselves when the leader isn't present. This is not a new idea. Lao-tzu, the great Taoist philosopher, said that the leader's role is ultimately to help people learn to lead themselves. This principle is the foundation of success for every distance manager.

Distance Managers Aren't Supervisors

How do you watch over someone you can't see? Even if the traditional role of supervision is desirable, it just isn't practical when the people to be supervised are located all over the map. This is often a difficult lesson that managers must learn as they progress up the corporate ladder. Confirms Roger Herman, CEO of the Herman Group, "Managing someone you can't see is considerably different than walking around the cubicle wall to see if they're there at eight in the morning."[3]

The Boundary Manager

We have written extensively about the role of leaders in empowered organizations.[4] Please allow us a brief summary of our findings as they apply to the distance manager. One of the best ways to describe the overall role of the distance manager is as a *boundary manager.* As you can see in Figure 1.1, the large circle in this figure represents the *team boundary.* The boundary is simply the make-believe line that differentiates the team from the environment surrounding it. The distance leader manages that boundary. What does that mean? Let's review a little organization theory to establish a common point of reference, and then we will answer that question.

Teams Are Open Systems

Figure 1.2 adds some things to the picture of the team we looked at earlier. Team members must take *inputs* (like raw materials or information) of some sort and transform them into desirable *outputs* (like products or

The Team's Environment
(All the things outside of the team itself)

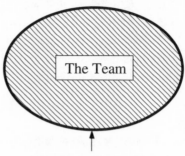

The Team

The Team Boundary

Figure 1.1   The Team Boundary
Adapted from *Leading Self-Directed Work Teams* by Kimball Fisher, used with permission

services). A special project team, for example, may be responsible for turning a problem (input) into a solution (output). A new-product development team turns ideas (input) into designs (output). A sales team turns customer interest (input) into orders (output). To do these things the teams add value to the inputs (change, assemble, organize, edit, etc.). This is called the *transformation* or *throughput* part of the operation. Figure 1.3 shows that outside the organization boundary is the *environment* (customers, competitors, other teams, etc.). Social scientists call this way of looking at organizations *open systems theory.*[5]

Teams Manage Inside the Boundary

Now let's get back to the original question: What does it mean to be a boundary manager? Traditional supervision usually focuses attention on the day-to-day transforming process or throughput portion of the team's responsibilities. Traditional managers make work assignments, schedule vacations, authorize expenditures, and so forth. But boundary managers teach the team to do that themselves, and then they work on boundary issues.

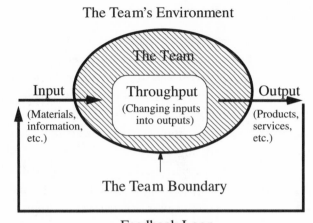

Figure 1.2   The Team as an Open System
Adapted from *Leading Self-Directed Work Teams* by
Kimball Fisher, used with permission

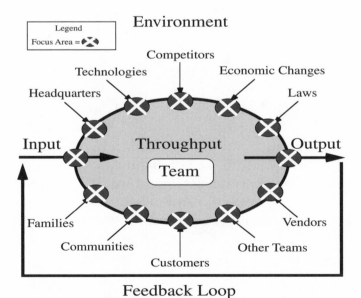

Figure 1.3   The Boundary Manager Focus Areas
Adapted from *Leading Self-Directed Work Teams* by Kimball
Fisher, used with permission

Distance Leaders Manage the Boundary

The distance manager focuses on the environment surrounding the team. Rather than spending his or her primary energy on the throughput process, the leader focuses more attention on interface problems with other teams, customer and vendor interactions, dealing with corporate groups, assessing competitors and market opportunities, working on legal or community issues of importance, forecasting new technologies, building communication bridges between team members and with other groups, forging important alliances, bringing training and development opportunities into the team, and so forth (see Figures 1.3 and 1.4). Those are the things at the boundary of the organization (represented in the figure by the circle). As a boundary manager, the distance leader manages these elements in the team's environment in a way that positively affects the team's ability to be successful—as Loewe did when he helped the team solve the problem between them and the customer.

Supervisors Work in the System, Boundary Managers Work on the System

Traditional supervisors usually work *in* the system, but boundary managers work *on* the system instead. That means working on things that affect the ability of the operation to be successful. Boundary managers assume that team members are already doing the best they can within the constraints of the system in which they are working. So they focus on improving or redesigning the system itself. In the short case study that opens this chapter, for example, Doug Loewe might take the solution to the customer problem one step further. The boundary manager asks, "Is there something in the system that makes team members act the way they do?" Perhaps the root cause of the lack of collaboration in the Loewe case was a reward system that gave salespeople commissions only for the sales they closed by themselves. If this were the case, the boundary manager may work to modify the commission system to encourage rather than discourage sharing and collaboration.

Seven Competencies of Boundary Managers

As we have mentioned, the overall role of the distance manager is to manage the team boundary. This includes a number of things. Bound-

---

Sample Boundary Tasks

Introducing team members to key external contacts

Buffering the team from corporate pressure

Bringing in information from headquarters

Evaluating market trends

Anticipating technology shifts

Building communication linkages between team members

Bringing in customer feedback

Forging alliances

Solving problems between teams or individuals

Bringing in technical training

Getting resources for the team

Bringing in concerned citizens to discuss community problems

Evaluating competitive offerings for similar products and services

Building systems for direct data links to and from customers/vendors

---

Figure 1.4   Examples of Boundary Manager Tasks
Adapted from *Leading Self-Directed Work Teams* by Kimball Fisher, used with permission

ary managers, for example, often play the role of translator as they try to help team members comprehend the fuzzy and chaotic reality of the outside world. They also block certain disruptions from entering the team, shielding it from inappropriate distractions or unnecessary confusion. Eric Ecklund, a member of the marketing and sales organization for Xerox, notes, for example, that one of the things his manager does that helps Ecklund and other team members significantly is to take the dozens of corporate e-mails they used to receive daily and filter out the ones that don't really affect them directly. Buffering members from these well-intentioned interruptions allows them to spend more time on sales and less on administrative responsibilities.

Effective distance managers possess a number of generic attributes, such as a clear understanding of what it takes to be successful, excellent oral and written communication abilities, and a strong interpersonal and technical skill base consistent with the organization's culture. As we interviewed distance leaders and their team members about the core competencies necessary for successful distance leadership, however, a few things turned up consistently as crucial to the effectiveness of virtual team leadership. We have written a great deal about these types of competencies for organizational leaders and were surprised to find that though the relative priorities or methodologies may differ, distance managers require the same behavior as other leaders we have studied. We expected to uncover new competencies specifically geared to distance management. Instead we found that—at least at the level of generally required behavior—distance managers must be competent in the same leadership activities as other effective managers. They:

1. Articulate a vision for the organization
2. Get good results
3. Actively facilitate and develop team members
4. Aggressively eliminate barriers to team effectiveness
5. Understand and communicate business and customer needs
6. Effectively coach individuals and teams
7. Set a personal example

These behaviors can be developed into seven clusters of competencies which further clarify the required skills for a successful distance leader (see Figure 1.5):

1. Leader
2. Results catalyst
3. Facilitator
4. Barrier buster
5. Business analyzer
6. Coach
7. Living example

What do these clusters mean? Let's start at the center of the model and work around it counterclockwise. As you will notice in the following examples, distance managers may need to use different technologies and techniques than their peers who manage co-located teams. Although the general competency is the same, the method for executing the competency may be unique in distance management.

1. The *leader* unleashes energy and enthusiasm by creating a vision that others find inspiring and motivating.[6] For example, distance

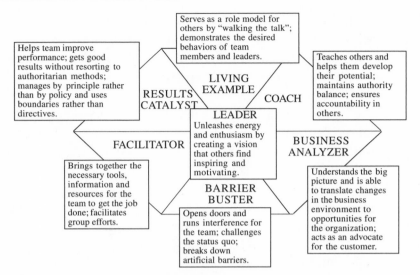

Figure 1.5   The Team Leader Role

executives like Steve Jobs, the two-time CEO of Apple Computer, Bill Gates, the cofounder of Microsoft, or Jeff Bezos of Amazon .com, were able to motivate remarkable accomplishments by creating a vision of a new world for their workforce.

But this competency isn't just for distance executives. The distance project managers, sales managers, and product development managers we interviewed showed us that leadership vision isn't limited to the top level of an organization. Anyone can and should have a picture of what is possible for the team they lead. A powerful vision of accomplishment transcends the distance caused by space, time, or culture and focuses everyone on a common cause.

2. The *results catalyst* helps the team improve performance, gets good results without resorting to authoritarian methods, manages by principle rather than by policy, and uses boundaries rather than directives. One of the most powerful competencies of the distance leader is the ability to focus people on getting good results. As we reviewed several distance management failures, for example, we found that they were seldom due to inappropriate use of technology. More often than not, distance management failures resulted from leaders taking their eye off the ball and focusing instead on things like pet projects or personal ego satisfaction. Ironically, some of the problems were

attributed to them being more interested in authoritarian methods than in good results. For example, a vice president of a major corporation once confessed to one of the authors that he favored compliance from his subordinates over results. It showed in his operation.

The bottom line is the bottom line. Organizations that don't deliver don't survive. But the *way* you deliver results is important, too. Distance managers who are good at managing by principle rather than by policy (a competency that has been taught to Procter and Gamble leaders for decades) and at using boundaries rather than directives (a common practice in companies like Weyerhaeuser and Hewlett-Packard) are normally more effective than those who get results by using a more autocratic approach. "It makes more sense to *empower* people to get good results than to try to *force* them to get them," commented one distance leader. "But you have got to deliver the results."

3. The *facilitator* brings together the necessary tools, information, and resources for the team to get the job done, and facilitates group efforts. Distance managers rely heavily on things like information and digital communication networks to substitute for their personal presence. For example, at WebSentric, a company that provides Web meeting support, founder and CEO Bill Barhydt has found that using WebSentric's own service in between face-to-face interactions allows him to accomplish things that would otherwise require him to be present to communicate product updates, customer needs, and technology challenges to off-site employees. Barhydt and his senior managers also rely heavily on their intranet as a way to demonstrate product revisions, share sales data, and communicate company direction. As a facilitator, distance leader Barhydt made significant investments both in these types of tools and in the time necessary to keep them updated. Why? He sees them as a critical way to facilitate employee involvement and communication.

4. The *barrier buster* opens doors and runs interference for the team, challenges the status quo, and breaks down artificial barriers to the team's performance. When Lynn Buchanan, a training manager at Weyerhaeuser Company, ran into difficulties in providing coaching support to widely distributed teams, she found a way to

overcome the barrier of costs associated with travel expenses to bring everyone together. Since it wasn't the kind of event that actually required people to physically be together, she partnered with some developers at Hewlett-Packard to come up with a way to deliver real-time coaching over the Web. She had the subject matter expert join in from Palo Alto, California, a group of people attend at the Weyerhaeuser headquarters in Federal Way (near Seattle), and then about 10 additional people join the discussion from 10 other locations. The subject matter expert (coach) was able to show overheads, draw ideas on a white board, and capture input using the third-party site capabilities at Hewlett-Packard.

5. The *business analyzer* understands the big picture, is able to translate changes in the business environment into opportunities for the organization, and acts as an advocate for the customer. Business focus is important to any organization, but it is especially important to virtual teams. These operations have a more significant risk of becoming disconnected from others in the company. They are also prone to focus time and energy on the topics that are of most importance to their particular site rather than to the overall business.

   Xerox and Chevron and a host of other organizations have found that a combination of intranet information and virtual town hall meetings via videoconferencing are useful for keeping people focused on the big picture. It often takes even more leadership intervention. Companies including Procter and Gamble, Hewlett-Packard, General Motors, Weyerhaeuser, and Chevron engage in periodic organizational redesign activities to change reporting relationships, pay systems, jobs, functions, and other elements of the company teams so that they emphasize integrated business performance over isolated pockets of excellence.

6. The *coach* teaches others and helps them develop their potential, maintains an appropriate authority balance, and ensures accountability in others. Certain distance leaders in Arco, for example, regularly engage in performance discussions with team members via videoconferencing. This ongoing coaching combined with face-to-face performance reviews provides a powerful opportunity for developing potential and ensuring accountability.

Accountability systems such as the star point method used at companies like Chevron and Owens Corning are also helpful coaching tools.[7] Star point systems identify certain results areas (e.g., cost savings, quality, speed, customer satisfaction) that are assigned to a particular team member to champion. This reduces reliance on the distance manager, distributes responsibilities among team members, and helps focus people on business issues rather than just the accomplishment of their jobs. More on these types of coaching recommendations can be found in Chapter 5, "The Distance Coach: Getting Peak Performance."

7. The *living example* serves as a role model for others by "walking the talk" and demonstrating the desired behaviors of team members and leaders. Virtual "walking the talk" includes a number of activities that can be practiced by distance leaders. For example, although the distance leader has few opportunities to set an example of how to act around the office, he or she can set an example of how to work with customers by inviting team members to join him or her on sales calls or other activities, as illustrated by Doug Loewe at the beginning of this chapter. While the distance leader can't regularly demonstrate proper meeting behavior, he or she can model things such as appropriate virtual meeting behavior, Internet etiquette, and e-mail usage.

Summary

Being a distance manager requires some special perspectives and techniques that are very different from the traditional roles of supervision we have seen in the past. Supervisory roles have been played by leaders at all levels in the corporation, not just by the first level. But they must change as one becomes a distance manager. While supervisors work *in* the system, distance managers work *on* the system instead. As boundary managers they perform responsibilities at the interface between the team and the team's environment. This allows the distance manager to help the teams stay focused on the big picture instead of becoming mired in the day-to-day throughput tasks for which the teams now have primary responsibility. It also allows distance managers to get needed resources and information from outside of the team.

We have found that successful boundary managers possess a number of general attributes and skills. They have highly developed competencies in the areas of leadership, getting results, facilitation, barrier busting, business analysis, coaching, and setting an example. Without skills in these areas, distance managers are not likely to be successful.

Because these competencies are so important to the distance manager, they will be examined in more detail in later chapters. We will provide practical tips and examples for things such as coaching from a distance and motivating by vision.

References

1. Doug Loewe, "Long-distance manager," *Sales and Marketing Management,* October 1994 v146 n11 p. 25(1). Quotes used with permission.
2. Ibid.
3. Lin Grensing-Pophal, "Training Supervisors to Manage Teleworkers," *HR Magazine,* Jan 1999 v44 il p67(5). Reprinted with the permission of *HR Magazine,* published by the Society for Human Resource Management, Alexandria, Virginia.
4. See our book, *The Distributed Mind: Achieving High Performance Through the Collective Intelligence of Knowledge Work Teams* (AMACOM 1998), and Kimball's book *Leading Self-Directed Work Teams* (revised and expanded edition) New York: McGraw-Hill, 1999.
5. David Hanna, *Designing Organizations for High Performance* Reading, Massachusetts: Addison-Wesley O.D. Series, 1988. Hanna does a nice job explaining open systems theory in this book. The original concept is usually attributed to Ludwig von Bertalanffy, "The Theory of Open Systems in Physics and Biology," *Science,* 111, 1950, pp. 23–28.
6. These descriptions and the "team leader role" model are part of the Fisher Group "Leadership Skills" training program © 1999 by The Fisher Group, Inc. All rights reserved. Used by permission.
7. Kimball Fisher, *Leading Self-Directed Teams* (revised edition) New York: McGraw-Hill, 1999. See Chapter 23, "Creating Accountability Systems for Teams."

Five Things That Cripple the Effectiveness of the Distance Manager

Leading a virtual team is difficult. The leader must provide structure, facilitate involvement, surface the personal dimension of the team members, recognize contributions, and be an involved sponsor. They role model the use of technology. They have to display disciplined follow-up. Virtual interactions are complex and very fatiguing.

Richard Thier, Manager,
Organization Effectiveness, Xerox

W HEN THE EXECUTIVE management of ARC, a consulting firm headquartered in Denver, Colorado, decided to make the whole company virtual, the transition required a tremendous amount of change. Although the managers had worked with selected virtual team members (consultants, trainers, and practitioners spread across the country) since the company's start-up in the late 1970s, they had always had a headquarters location where many of the consultants and managers maintained offices. The headquarters was more than just a place to meet in between client assignments; it was a symbol of their operation, a brick-and-mortar edifice that gave them a shared sense of identity.

When the managers decided to vacate their headquarters in 1997 to operate exclusively out of their homes and customer sites, team members and leaders experienced a sense of loss. One loss was the status that had come with the fancy trappings of the offices. Dennis Stratton, the CEO, found that leaders had to learn to relinquish many of the traditional methods of management that required physical interaction or "position power." He admits that for many leaders this was very difficult.[1]

But they were struck with a deeper, more profound loss as well. Randall Alford, one of the consultants, called the building a place where he and his associates could find "community." Although they faced challenges implementing the information and communication technology systems that would allow them to link with each other through e-mail, voice mail, and shared files, the bigger challenge—*the far bigger challenge*—was to find a way to recreate the sense of purpose and community they had enjoyed with the building. Alford notes that most managers think of this change as a technological event rather than a human event. That's a mistake. Team members missed the interaction with others; they felt lonely and isolated at home; and they found it more difficult to coordinate activities over the narrower bandwidth of electronic communication systems that replaced almost all of the face-to-face meetings.

ARC's senior managers had to do a number of things to overcome these obstacles. As previously mentioned, to bridge time and space they instituted appropriate communication technologies and ensured that people knew how to use them effectively. This is an example of the facilitator competency introduced in Chapter 1. But as an example of the leadership competency (and as a way to bridge the culture distance created by the abandonment of their building), they also encouraged informal chat room–type electronic communication between team members. Consultants shared their fears and frustrations during these interchanges, and eventually re-created a sense of community and identity. Although some leaders initially thought the interchanges were a waste of time, they later realized the important role the discussions played in creating a more homogeneous work culture.

As the ARC story demonstrates, virtual teams need effective leadership to surmount several challenges. Distance managers tell us that five things, in particular, can cripple your effectiveness: (1) either autocratic or abdication behavior, (2) poor virtual team start-ups, (3) unclear roles and responsibilities, (4) starving teams of resources, and (5) lack of either social and/or technical infrastructure (see Figure 2.1). The first of these five things refers to general management behavior and the last four are specific activities required to make distance teams successful. Let's consider each of them in turn.

Avoiding Autocratic Behavior

As was already mentioned in chapter 1, autocratic behavior—the staple of the traditional supervisor—impedes distance teams. Savvy leaders of organizations have known this for years.

Consider a brief but not unusual example. A few years ago Amoco and Shell Oil combined resources to create a company called Altura,

1. DON'T be autocratic nor an abdicator.	1. DO be a leader, results catalyst, facilitator, barrier buster, business analyzer, coach, and living example.
2. DON'T allow poor team start-ups.	2. DO "purpose" the team well.
3. DON'T allow unclear roles and responsibilities to confuse people.	3. DO help everyone understand what each person does and needs from others.
4. DON'T starve teams of resources.	4. DO get them the tools, time, and budget necessary to succeed.
5. DON'T forget to create both social and technical infrastructure.	5. DO install the systems, tools, protocols, and training for success.

Figure 2.1   Five Dos and Don'ts for Distance Managers

which specializes in recovering oil from depleted wells. Using employees, technologies, and capital from each company, they were able to do together what neither had been able to do separately: find cost-effective ways to more efficiently use oil-producing resources.

Charlie Wagner, a plant management team leader for Altura, remembers a virtual team he sponsored early in the history of the company. "The team leader," he recalls, "was an engineer who was extremely intelligent. He loved making decisions. He became good at manipulating the team into coming up with the decisions he thought were best. After a while, the team caught on and became resentful even though most of the decisions that were made were probably good ones."

Team effectiveness and productivity diminished as people came to feel that they had little say in the project. After being confronted by the team, the team leader recognized that he enjoyed being an individual technical contributor more than a team leader. Altura transferred him to a different assignment. He still has a lot of influence, but he no longer serves as a leader of others. "He admitted he was in the wrong role," says Charlie. Autocratic leaders, even nice or intelligent ones, are rarely successful with virtual teams, which depend on each individual to willingly contribute his or her full effort. Once people feel that you really don't want their participation, they'll stop giving it.

Good distance managers tell us is that even the perception of autocracy can torpedo your effectiveness. Seemingly innocuous or even well-intended behavior can sometimes be seen as autocratic simply because it is unilaterally imposed without having clearly perceived benefits to the team as a whole.

Some leaders, for example, in an attempt to keep themselves informed, impose a reporting requirement on team members that is often perceived as autocratic. Jim Hoffman is the leader of a virtual team of consultants that offers pro bono support to the middle schools located in the communities in which their employer, International Paper, has a mill (see Chapter 22, "The Distance Project Manager," for a detailed description of this team). Since the consultants are spread all over the country, it has been difficult for Hoffman to stay abreast of their work. During an attempt to impose a communication process on team members that would keep him better informed but require extra work for them, the consultants told him that they felt the process added little value and was an administrative (nice words for autocratically imposed) burden.

Always sensitive to the needs of the team, Hoffman backed off his position lest he lose the collegial respect that he felt was necessary in this group of highly educated professionals. He found other ways to stay informed that require a bit more work for him but preserve the nonautocratic posture that increases the commitment and motivation of the consultants. "Live and learn," he says.

There are lots of ways that managers can be seen as autocratic. Focusing too much energy on the means (throughput) rather than the ends (outputs) of the work commonly leads to this problem. When the team itself requires throughput monitoring to accomplish its task, that's one thing; but when the information gathering is mandated by managers for the sole benefit of the manager, it actually causes more problems than it solves.

In many circumstances, for example, people have discovered that the process of frequently submitting electronic status reports for distance managers costs *significantly* more in lost time and salaries than the value of any improvements that result from the process. Good distance managers avoid this trap. If such frequent reporting really is necessary, consider something like posting status reports on a public electronic bulletin board. This appears less authoritarian because everybody can see what everybody else is doing, which helps other team members stay informed along with the manager. Other distance managers have eliminated the practice of regular status reports altogether, preferring communication driven by project need instead of artificial calendar dates or management preferences.

Abdication

The answer to avoiding autocracy, however, isn't to be among the missing. Some well-intended leaders have left their teams alone without intervention when they saw them faltering. Other managers, in the name of industrial democracy, have bogged teams down by forcing them to participate in every little decision. "Let the team figure it out on their own," or "I shouldn't interfere," may be something the distance manager says on occasion to help his or her team build ownership, competence, or confidence, but it fails terribly as a regular management mantra. We have written about this popular misconception as the "myth of the marshmallow manager."[2] Leaders who believe their role is to be sweet and sticky won't survive the rigors of distance management requirements. They'll get toasted.

Good distance managers strike a balance between autocracy and abdication. To assume that abdication is an acceptable role of leaders is to concede that there really is no need for distance managers at all. Our experience is quite the opposite. Although the role of the distance manager is not to be autocratic, it is to provide the vision, coaching, and support that is mentioned in the seven leadership competencies we introduced in Chapter 1. In fact, if the choice comes down to autocracy or abdication, most of the leaders we interviewed would choose autocracy. It is much more difficult to fill the vacuum left by an abdicating leader than to repair the damage done by an autocratic but otherwise competent one.

Developing Moral Authority

Rather than an authority based on position or title, effective distance managers rely on the authority that comes from purpose, knowledge, or wisdom. This almost becomes a type of moral authority that supersedes rank and earns genuine respect from others. It certainly is the only kind of authority that would work for a Mahatma Gandhi, a Martin Luther King, Jr., or a Nelson Mandela. In spite of the dramatic differences between the lives of these leaders, including differences in time, space, and culture, there were remarkable similarities as well. Each led a campaign for equality (Indian independence, U.S. civil rights, and abolition of South African apartheid, respectively) and shared some common values about methodology (each preferred non-violent means despite intense personal and organizational persecution). With that purpose and those values came an authority higher than that which comes from title alone.

In movements where firing followers is not an option, the wisdom of this approach is obvious. Parallels are clear to the distance manager who leads people from multiple organizations and who therefore cannot resort to either the carrot or the stick as a means of motivation. But even to the distance manager who can use formal sanctions and rewards, using what we call the *purposing* of an organization can bring a whole deeper level of commitment and energy than is otherwise possible.

Psychologists have told us for years that performance that comes from fears or threats (e.g., getting fired) or even from hopes of rewards (e.g., getting raises/promotions) is neither as profound nor as sustainable as performance that comes from an internally generated commitment to accomplish something the person believes is inherently worthwhile. Look at Olympic athletes, especially those in sports where lucrative professional careers or endorsements aren't a distracting factor. What motivates the athlete is a personal drive to excel that far exceeds the motivation derived from most other sources.

Poor Start-Ups

The second thing that can cripple your effectiveness as a distance manager is a poor virtual team start-up. Of all the advice we received from leaders and team members when we asked the question, "What can leaders do to help virtual teams be more effective?" the most common tip was, "Do a good face-to-face start-up." Says Steven Gibbons, former president of the Association for Quality and Participation, "You have to start off with some face-to-face time to create a bond and develop agreements on how you are going to work together." Gibbons understands this not only from his experience at work but also from that gained as the president of a very large professional organization. "We were actually more productive as an executive board when we were working electronically than when we worked together in person," notes Gibbons. "We liked each other so much that we tended to spend more time socializing than working when we were together. But because we had established such a strong bond, we were able to work virtually much more effectively."

Nothing is more vital for virtual team effectiveness than a start-up activity where team members can meet each other, do some team building, develop goals and measures, and clarify roles and responsibilities. In Chapters 6 ("Distance Team Building: Practical Tips for Building Effective Teams") and 12 ("The Necessity of Face to Face Meetings") we will discuss this kind of start-up in more detail. If you want to review this now, skip forward to these chapters and then rejoin us where you left off.

Without a successful start-up, virtual teams can often flounder for the duration of their existence. If you invest in no other activity for your team, get it off to a good start. Likewise, long-standing teams, or teams that for whatever reason never had a formal start-up, will usually benefit from a "restart" activity.

Unclear Roles and Responsibilities

One of the tasks of a good start-up meeting is to clarify roles and responsibilities. This is also something good distance managers help teams negotiate and renegotiate throughout the duration of the team. In our consulting team, for example, we go through a simple but important discussion about twice a year. We identify the key assignments of each team member, collect expectations from everybody about how those assignments need to be performed, and identify cross-training requirements for everyone. Doing this accomplishes a couple of things. First, it helps clarify who is responsible for what, eliminating overlapping responsibilities and exposing gaps that need to be filled. Second, it does this in a way that is neither autocratic nor abdicating. As leaders we make sure the meeting happens and often play a major role in facilitating it. But the work expectations come from everyone, not just the leaders. Regardless of hierarchical position, everyone gets to say, "Here is what I need from you to get my work done." Everyone on the team finds this useful.

Follow-up sessions necessary to renegotiate roles and responsibilities can usually be done virtually. But be warned: *What can be a powerful intervention face-to-face can quickly devolve into hurt feelings or apathy without at least a recent memory of personal physical presence.* There are things you can say to someone face-to-face, for example, that cannot be said in an e-mail, where you can't develop a context or build on a positive relationship. Constructive feedback is more likely to be helpful in person than virtually.

Starving Teams of Resources

The fourth thing that can cripple your effectiveness as a distance manager is to allow the team to be starved of necessary resources. Although leaders seldom do this intentionally, sometimes a lack of understanding of remote needs, or a desire to impose their own opinions on distance team members may create either a mismatch or a paucity of important resources. At a minimum, team members need the tools to do their work to the satisfaction of their customers. This of course varies according to your operation. But because team members are off-site they also need good information and communication systems. This requires a way for them to interact effectively with you and with each other electronically.

The major hardware problems people normally have with these resource setups are compatibility, bandwidth, and memory. Applications with video, in particular, require much more bandwidth and memory than most shared files or many other types of groupware do. But getting the right boxes and links is the easy part. The biggest issues (read this as either "problems" or "opportunities" depending on whether you are a pessimist or an optimist) are normally software- and user-related. See the chapters in Part III: "The Distance Technology Handbook," for more information.

Like in any other team, the key resources that team members need in virtual environments are time and money. You might, in fact, argue that the fundamental function of management is to allocate scarce resources to their best advantage. No one has all the time and money they want. But differential advantage goes to those who figure out what the highest leverage resources are and how to deploy them successfully. This can seldom be done unilaterally from afar. Distance managers normally engage their teams in discussions about how to prioritize constrained budgets, equipment, and personnel to get maximum sustainable gains. As difficult as it sounds, some virtual sales groups now work together to determine everyone's territory and quotas. Once a sacred right of the sales leader, these discussions on sensitive resource allocations can produce better overall results than the autocratic alternative, if teams are sufficiently trained and motivated.

Lack of Social and/or Technical Infrastructure

The final killer for the distance manager is a lack of social and/or technical infrastructure. Infrastructure in a country is the system of freeways, mass transit, bridges, power plants, telephone lines and towers, and so forth. It facilitates travel, communication, and energy use by linking places together and by providing basic utilities. Although these systems often exist quietly in the background, they enable effective interaction of the citizens. Without them there is little economic progress.

Similarly, organizations create infrastructures. Technical infrastructures include things like telecommunications, computer networks, intranets, Internet access, videoconference equipment, software, and so forth. The social infrastructure relates to systems and processes for organizing and leading people, such as organizational configurations, pay systems, appraisal and performance management processes, charters, training systems, and so forth.

Infrastructure Can Substitute for Hierarchy

Social and technical infrastructures are important for effective operation of organizations. Without these systems teams would be thrown into chaos, not competitiveness. Like it or not, in most organizations the much-maligned Industrial Age concepts of hierarchy and bureaucracy have performed an important coordination function that must still somehow be performed in the virtual workplace. A number of companies have reported problems when hierarchical controls (e.g., management authorizations, policies, procedures) are withdrawn from teams prematurely without anything to replace the clarity and direction that those controls previously provided. Distance managers ensure that teams have these substitutions for hierarchy in place. These substitutions are more important in distance teams than in co-located ones because distance team members (minus your frequent presence) are more likely to assume ill (autocratic) intent on your part than are co-located teams. It's just human nature.

Socio-Technical Systems (STS)

Just after World War II, researchers from the Tavistock Institute in London made an important discovery. Commissioned by the government to find cost-effective ways to rebuild the industrial base of the United Kingdom, they demonstrated that organizations that had both good technical systems *and* good social systems significantly outperformed those operations without strong infrastructure in both categories. Englishman Eric Trist and his other social scientist colleagues (including Australian Fred Emery) called these effective organizations *socio-technical systems.* They are considered by most organizational historians to be the fathers of the modern team-based high-performance work organization.

What is the bottom line? Excellence in either the technical or human side of business is never enough. There are countless stories of virtual teams that have failed in spite of the fact that they had superb communication technology. Conversely, teams with excellent social systems without the necessary technologies to work together are doomed. Good distance managers ensure that the teams have both.

Summary

Good distance managers avoid five things that can cripple their effectiveness: (1) either autocratic or abdication behavior, (2) poor virtual team start-ups, (3) unclear roles and responsibilities, (4) starving teams of resources, and (5) lack of either social and/or technical infrastructure. They know that developing a type of moral authority; properly purposing teams; clearly delineating roles and responsibilities; providing time, budget, and other resources; and developing both social and technical infrastructure as a substitution for hierarchy are essential to distance leadership.

References

1. Randall J. Alford, "Going Virtual, Getting Real," *Training and Development,* Jan 1999 v53 il p 34(1).
2. Kimball Fisher, *Leading Self-Directed Work Teams* (revised and expanded edition) New York: McGraw-Hill, 1999.

3

What Employees Want from a Distance Manager

What I want from a virtual team manager is to keep me informed. That's something my manager is really good at. He has the responsibility of managing a human resources team where the team members are on the road most of the time. They operate from several locations spread across the country. Something that he does that we all really appreciate is send us a weekly correspondence with key issues and facts in summary form.

Mike Kuczwara, Senior Human Resources Manager
Procter & Gamble

T HE AUTHORS WOULD like to share a personal (and somewhat embarrassing) example of how easy it is to make mistakes as distance managers. Not too long ago we experienced some challenges associated with the shipping and retrieving of training materials to and from some of our clients. Our team is composed of both consultants (who are normally on the road and/or located in other states from our corporate office in Oregon) and customer service and materials coordinators (who are located at the corporate office location). As company leaders, we immediately diagnosed the problem and recommended what we thought was the appropriate solution: a very thorough tracking system we created. This would give us the confidence that things were under control when we and the other consultants were on the road.

Once we instructed the materials coordinator on how to implement the solution, we assumed that it was fixed. Not long afterward, however, the problem resurfaced, and materials from another client site were somehow misplaced. Frustrated, we called a special team meeting to resolve the problem before it affected any more clients. During the meeting, we came to realize that we had used the very approach we had cautioned our clients against. For some time we had recommended that managers "share the problem, not the solution" as a way to empower others. But instead we had only shared our solution and asked people to implement it. We controlled the *people* (by inferring blame and demanding that our idea be implemented) instead of the *process* (discussing our ideas with others and focusing on the tools and techniques necessary for fixing the problem).

We apologized for mandating a solution and began to control the process instead. We described the problem and invited the materials coordinator to develop a new work process of her choosing that would solve it. The coordinator created a new, less cumbersome tracking system that did just that. The problem went away and the coordinator felt that she had been empowered to solve it. Where before she had just been implementing someone else's solution, she now had a feeling of ownership for implementing and maintaining her own solution to the problem (which we discovered in the discussion, by the way, was more due to our lack of communication with the home office than, as we had assumed, to the material coordinator's lack of attention to detail).

The authors discovered how easy it is to slip back into controlling the person instead of managing the machines, techniques, or series of steps necessary to accomplish the work. Our new mantra at work is, "We need a better process," instead of something like, "Who made the mistake?" As a consequence, virtual team members have created work processes that range from an accountability system to make sure that assignments are followed up on, to a new process for delivering team training over the Internet. These work processes provide direction and focus for the work whether we are on-site or not.

How Do You Control Distance Workers?

"My biggest concern," confided one distance leader, "is that they won't be productive when I'm not there. How do you control off-site employees?" The saying, "When the cat's away, the mice will play," has been quoted to us many times by concerned distance managers. We are also embarrassed to confess that we have sometimes felt this ourselves.

As our story at the start of the chapter demonstrates, it may be this very way of thinking that lessens the distance manager's ability to maintain appropriate control of an off-site workforce. Thinking that workers need to be controlled often causes the distance leader to over-control through policies and procedures that can actually cause the problem the leader so assiduously wants to avoid.

Distance workers often feel distrusted or inadequate if their work environment is based on hierarchically generated control. This affects their work negatively. When the distance worker feels overcontrolled by management, he or she tends to act in one of the following ways: (1) they become compliant and dependent on the manager; (2) they resist the controls and find ways to play games to get around them; or (3) they become apathetic. None of these states promotes the highest level of employee performance.

If you ask team members what they want from a distance manager, you seldom hear them ask for more autocracy, hierarchy, or bureaucracy. More clarity, yes; definite priorities, sure; a sense of direction, absolutely. But more than the traditional management attributes of planning, organizing, directing, and controlling, team members want the sort of coaching and facilitation that comes from someone who sees his or her job as *supporting* rather than *directing* the team. They probably want the same things from you that you want from your leader.

Specifically, we consistently hear team members make 10 requests of their leaders: (1) coordination rather than control, (2) accessibility rather than either inaccessibility or omnipresence, (3) information without overload, (4) feedback instead of advice, (5) fairness over favoritism, (6) decisiveness but not intrusive supervision, (7) honesty rather than manipulation, (8) concern for their development over apathy, (9) community building over mere coordinated isolation, and (10) respect rather than paternalism or condescension. These are not listed in any particular order; almost all of the expectations were rated as being important to employees who talked to us about distance leadership. Let's review these expectations (see Figure 3.1).

Coordination Rather than Control

The first expectation is that the distance manager exercise coordination, not control. While team members appreciate attempts at coordination, they normally chafe under what they perceive to be control. Ironically, the best control of the off-site office is the control imposed from within (self-control) rather than from outside (manager-imposed) anyway. So the question is, "How do you encourage self-control without being controlling?" According to Harvard professor Richard Walton, you do it by changing management paradigms from a control orientation to what he calls the *commitment paradigm*.[1] We think he's

---

1. Coordination rather than control
2. Accessibility rather than inaccessibility or omnipresence
3. Information without overload
4. Feedback instead of advice
5. Fairness over favoritism
6. Decisiveness but not intrusive supervision
7. Honesty rather than manipulation
8. Concern for development over apathy
9. Community building over coordinated isolation
10. Respect rather than paternalism or condescension

Figure 3.1   Ten Things Employees Want from a Distance Manager

right. See Figure 3.2 for examples of the difference between the control and commitment paradigms.

This is a difficult tightrope to walk. Having too many policies, for example, is often perceived as unnecessary control, while having too few is seen as poor coordination. The key to proper balance is to stay well-connected to team members. If you hear things like, "We really feel like our hands are tied," or, "You haven't given us much choice here," you have probably erred on the side of too much control. Under these conditions, team members generally will not accept ownership or accountability for their work (e.g., "I was just doing what you told me to do," or, "That's not my job."). If you hear things like, "What are our Paris teammates doing?" or, "We're confused because of the inconsistency in how people do things," you have probably erred on the side of not enough coordination. Under these conditions, productivity suffers.

Control Paradigm	Commitment Paradigm
Elicits compliance	Engenders commitment
Believes supervision is necessary	Believes education is necessary
Focuses on hierarchy	Focuses on customers
Bias for functional organizations	Bias for cross-functional organizations
Manages by policy	Manages by principle
Favors audit and enforcement processes	Favors learning processes
Believes in selective information sharing	Believes in open information sharing
Believes bosses should make decisions	Believes workers should make decisions
Emphasis on means	Emphasis on ends
Encourages hard work	Encourages balanced work/ personal life
Rewards conservative improvement	Rewards continuous improvement
Encourages agreement	Encourages thoughtful disagreement

Figure 3.2   Differences Between Management Paradigms
Adapted from *Leading Self-Directed Work Teams* by Kimball Fisher, used with permission

Being out of balance on either side (control or coordination) affects morale.

Accessibility Rather than Inaccessibility or Omnipresence

The second expectation is for the distance manager to be accessible. Even if you could be physically present all the time, team members would neither expect nor want you to. The desire for autonomy in most distance employees is very high. "But," says Mark Nyman, who is Director of Business Transformation at MediaOne and who has worked with numerous virtual teams in different companies, "virtual team members want their leaders to be accessible. They want to know they can reach them when they need to." This doesn't mean that distance managers need to be on call 24 × 7, but it usually does mean that they carry personal communication devices such as cell phones or beepers a lot. It also means that they make the extra effort of telling team members when they are not accessible due to vacation, illness, or personal reasons. This extra courtesy creates a sort of virtual leadership presence that employees feel they have some control over.

Information Without Overload

The third expectation is for the distance manager to provide information without overload. If information is the lifeblood of virtual teams, the challenge for the distance manager is to give people what they need to sustain their health without unintentionally creating internal hemorrhaging from too much data. Keep them informed but not inundated. The right balance of information is extremely difficult to maintain, and it may differ significantly from team to team. What is too much information for one team ("We can't get anything done because we have too many meetings!") may be too little for another ("How do you expect us to get our work done when we don't know what is going on?"). Unfortunately, the technologies to facilitate information passing among team members can also inundate them with unnecessary detail or redundancy. When you *do* find the right balance, team members are very appreciative. For tips on how to deal with problems such as e-mail glut, see Chapter 18, "Management by E-Mail—Without Letting It Take Over Your Life."

Feedback Instead of Advice

The fourth expectation is feedback. People generally appreciate receiving skillfully delivered information about how they are doing. James Gautier is a member of the virtual team of middle school consultants introduced earlier. That team meets physically only a few times each year. "One thing I really appreciate," says Gautier, "is getting feedback. Sometimes one of the other consultants will sit in on a presentation I'm doing and tell me how they think it was received, or Jim (the team leader) will let me know how the teachers and administrators evaluated the session. That helps when you don't have your leader or peers around all the time."

"What most people dislike," adds Dee Oviatt, a consulting team member at Pioneer Hi-Bred International, "isn't getting negative feedback about their performance, it's getting inappropriate advice." While appropriate advice is helpful, inappropriate advice (e.g., not work-related, unsolicited, too superficial, or not based on a full understanding of the situation) can have a dramatic negative effect on morale. While people want mentoring, they don't want meddling. There is a difference.

How can you tell whether you're mentoring or meddling? Ask the team member. One way to avoid meddling is to wait for the teaching moment when an employee solicits advice. Another is to be careful about how you word things. Saying something like "Paul, your clients let me know that they loved your last visit because you really took the time to listen to their concerns; they'd like to see that more often," is better than, "Paul, you need to listen to your clients." One statement is feedback based on data or observation. The other is unsolicited advice. The problem with giving a lot of advice (especially general advice) as a distance manager is that the team members may wonder how you would be in a position to offer it when you aren't with them very often.

Fairness over Favoritism

The next expectation by virtual team members is to be treated fairly. Fairness generally ranks very high in surveys about employee expectations of their leaders. This is especially important in distance situations because perceived inequities are magnified over time and space.

Favoritism of any type can affect the productivity of distance workers. "Why should I work so hard," they rationalize, "when results count for less than whether the manager likes you or not?" In addition to steering clear of the obvious problems of allowing certain team members to be perceived as favorites (e.g. "He always gets the good assignments"), distance managers need to avoid being site-, time-, or culture-centric. It isn't fair, for example, if the same people always have to get out of bed for teleconferences. It isn't fair if people who don't speak English are always left to fend for themselves during meetings. It isn't fair if the same people always travel long distances for the face-to-face meetings. Distance managers assiduously avoid these inequities and are willing to share in the sacrifice required of members of a virtual team. That is part of being the living example mentioned in Chapter 1. If *you* aren't willing to take your turn getting up at night for a global meeting, or to come in on night shift, or to travel to a remote location for a meeting, why should your team members?

Decisiveness but Not Intrusive Supervision

The sixth expectation is that the distance manager exercise appropriate decisiveness. Team members don't want intrusive supervision, but they don't want you to be among the missing, either. When a leadership decision needs to be made, make it. Although team members want to be involved in decisions that affect the way they do their work, there are certain decisions that you need to make by yourself.

The most obvious example of this is disciplinary action. Few things are more demotivating to a team than when leaders don't resolve employee performance problems. Unresolved incompetence, perpetual lack of safe behaviors, unfulfilled customer requirements, or blatant individual problems such as dishonesty or sexual harassment can quickly derail a whole team—even at a distance. A good coach (another one of the key competencies noted in Chapter 1) knows how to work with people to help them improve. You might obtain additional information for your company's specific approaches to these kinds of problems through your human resources representative.

Although 360-degree feedback activities where peer feedback is received from other team members are becoming quite common, group disciplinary decisions are still unusual, particularly in virtual teams where the leader may have as much interaction with the team member as his or her non-co-located peers do. Do not abdicate these types of performance decisions.

Honesty Rather than Manipulation

Another clear expectation that team members have of their distance manager is honesty. In their research on employee expectations of leaders, Kouzes and Posner[2] found that the number one concern was honesty of leadership. We have heard similar expectations from numerous team members we have talked with. They don't want to be manipulated into false participation where the leader tries to get them to agree to his or her way of thinking. They also don't want sugarcoating. They certainly don't want things to be hidden from them. Honesty is the best policy, because it encourages trust and builds a culture of openness.

Concern for Development Versus Apathy

The eighth expectation is that the distance leader will train and develop the team members. This is especially important to employees who feel disconnected from the rest of the organization. Although perceptive employees realize that the days of employment security and company-driven career planning are gone, they do want to know that their leader genuinely cares about their professional development. Employees generally believe that organizations that focus time and energy on employee development are more likely to be successful, viable operations than those that don't. They are also happiest when they believe they are being groomed not only for their current role and responsibilities but for future assignments as well.

Team members expect that you will be concerned about getting them trained in three categories: (1) business training to better understand their customers, markets, competitors, and financials; (2) technical training to learn how to operate the technologies necessary for them to do their jobs; and (3) interpersonal training to work more effectively with you and their teammates in areas such as effective problem solving, decision making, conflict resolution, and giving and receiving feedback. Remember that classroom training isn't always the best way to develop these skills. The most effective learning is often derived from developmental project assignments or mentoring programs.

Community Building Versus Coordinated Isolation

The ninth expectation also has special importance to distance workers. Virtual team members often experience a feeling of isolation that comes from not working near the rest of their teammates and leaders. The most effective distance managers help them overcome these concerns through team-building activities and other community-building interventions like those mentioned in Chapter 9, "Overcoming the Isolation of the Satellite Office," and Chapter 10, "Managing Employees Who Work at Home." Helping these workers deal with their feelings of isolation requires more than connecting them electronically with you and their peers—that's only coordinated isolation. Building a team takes more effort. It takes work to clarify the team charter, establish operating guidelines, and get to know the other team members as more than an anonymous node on the team network. See Chapter 6, "Distance Team Building: Practical Tips for Building Effective Teams" for some tips.

Community building is more important than it appears at first blush. For example, one virtual team member confided to us that although the team she worked on was successful in accomplishing a major project on time and within budget, the personal toll was too great. "I would never do it again," she said. "It was too hard to receive feedback on my work from people I didn't know and consequently couldn't respect. My leader didn't handle it well. She only focused on getting the task done. We burned out. Our work could have been better. Just taking the time to help us get to know each other would have made the work go faster and better in the long run. I felt like a robot instead of a human member of a team."

Respect Versus Paternalism or Condescension

The team members' final expectation is to be respected. Respect is a basic human need. When it is absent in a society, people revolt. In a business they may become cynical, apathetic, or nonproductive. While they certainly do not want condescending behavior from their leaders, they also do not want the paternalism exhibited by many well-intended corporations. Unfortunately, both condescending behavior and paternalistic behavior send the same unintended message to the recipient: "You can't take care of yourself so I'm going to take care of you." Even in the best of circumstances this approach can create unhealthy dependence, lower self-esteem, and stunted self-initiative.

Summary

In this chapter we have reviewed 10 common requests that employees have for distance managers: (1) coordination rather than control, (2) accessibility rather than inaccessibility or omnipresence, (3) information without overload, (4) feedback instead of advice, (5) fairness over favoritism, (6) decisiveness but not intrusive supervision, (7) honesty rather than manipulation, (8) concern for their development over apathy, (9) community building over mere coordinated isolation, and (10) respect rather than paternalism or condescension. In later chapters we will focus more attention on some of the best practices in several of these areas. Controlling processes instead of people enables the distance manager to empower people. It is an approach more consistent with the commitment paradigm than the control paradigm and it helps the leader ensure that employees are productive whether or not the leader is present.

References

1. Richard Walton, "From Control to Commitment in the Workplace." *Harvard Business Review*, March–April 1985.
2. James M. Kouzes and Barry Z. Posner, *The Leadership Challenge: How to Get Extraordinary Things Done in Organizations*, San Francisco: Jossey-Bass, 1987. Copyright © 1987 James M. Kouzes. Reprinted by permission of Jossey-Bass, Inc., a subsidiary of John Wiley & Sons, Inc.

4

Six Types of Virtual Teams

We have 17,000 people dispersed in 2000 locations—none of which we own—in 43 states, serving 35,000 patients a day. And the question is, what are they all doing? Especially since each one could put me in jail each day. . . . We've found that after developing the technology to connect and communicate [to] dispersed personnel, the challenge is to develop the operating culture that allows for its utilization. Our culture is the only thing— except for our name—that connects all of these people in all of these units.[1]

John H. Foster, Chairman
NovaCare

V IRTUAL TEAMS TYPICALLY cross time, space, and organization boundaries.[2] Understanding these three variables is important in determining what kind of virtual teams you are leading and for helping you decide on appropriate actions to improve them. For example, a team that has members working in the same place at different times (such as a technical support service team working from the same bank of telephones, but with a day, afternoon, and night-shift crew) might be able to meet some of their communication needs by updating a large chart located in their office each shift. But a team distributed across multiple sites would need a different communication strategy.

Culture Is More Important than Organization

To help determine what kind of team you work with, let's look at a modified version of these three variables. We believe that what is important in addition to time and geographical separation is actually culture, rather than just organization. We have seen operations within the same organization, for example, that had special challenges associated with multiple cultures, while other virtual teams with participants from multiple companies were very homogeneous because the participants shared the exact same technical background. For this reason we will use the variables of time, distance, and *culture* to create a diagnostic model to help you work more effectively as a distance manager.

Obviously these variables are strongly related. Physicists tell us, for example, that space and time are actually part of the same continuum. This is easy to see if you imagine a widely dispersed team. If people are located in several geographies, then they will also be in different time zones as well. Thus, space-time is really one variable rather than two. Culture is also affected by space-time. The more distributed the team is in time and space the more likely they are to have a less homogeneous culture. But for the purposes of this book we will differentiate each of the variables.

Space, Time, or Culture Can Create Distance

The leaders we interviewed assured us that space, time, *or* culture can create distance. We've already discussed space in some detail, but consider time as something that creates another type of distance. When a team must function seamlessly around the clock, how do you ensure that information from one shift gets to the other ones? How can you ensure continuity, fairness, and appropriate standardization? How do best practices get coordinated? How do organization-wide problems get solved? How do you get real time input and buy-in from across an operation when important team members from other shifts or time zones are always home asleep?

What seems simple in what experts call a *synchronous* (same-time) environment can become a nightmare in an asynchronous one. Some teams have been known to erupt into near-violent disagreement over something as mundane as the timing of meetings. "Why does everything have to happen on day shift?" they ask. Or in operations with membership that spans multiple time zones, team members want to know who has to get up in the middle of the night or lose precious weekend time for an international teleconference. "Must the Europeans, Asians, and Africans always be the ones to accommodate their American partners?" they justifiably complain.

To make matters worse, space-time distance isn't the only kind of distance a leader must learn to bridge. Is the distance caused by cultural differences any less problematic? Ed Schein, an M.I.T. professor whose research focuses on organizational culture, has identified a myriad of problems that can come from this elusive characteristic. If we adapt a definition of culture from Schein, anything that falls into the category of a "learned behavior about how to work together" is culture.[3] This covers a broad spectrum ranging from organizational to language and ethnic norms. Gaps in these areas can create a great deal of distance.

At Procter & Gamble, where we worked before becoming consultants, for example, the marketing part of the company had a very different type of culture than the manufacturing part of the company did. Inside of the manufacturing part of the company there were subcultures. Unionized operations were different than nonunion plants. Maintenance organizations within a plant were distinct from operations. Night-shift culture was different than day-shift culture. Office workers were different than people on the floor. In some cases there were distinct cultural differences on the same team.

Obviously, teams that cross countries often find subtle but important communication challenges caused by very distinct geographical cultures. At the risk of perpetuating stereotypes, consider what some people have reported to us about working on global teams. South Americans on the project may see timelines as approximate, while Germans may view them as precise, even though both sit through the same discussion in the same language at the same time. Asians may smile and nod their heads when asked if they agree to something that they know they cannot later support, because the rudeness of overt disagreement is culturally intolerable. North Americans may run roughshod over respected but time-consuming practices of other cultures. This short-term efficiency focus may backfire in the long term as it erodes trust and employee commitment.

Sometimes the biggest chasm of all the distance manager faces is the cultural distance between team members.

A Model to Represent Six Types of Virtual Teams

Imagine that each variable is on its own continuum ranging from the same (same time, same space, same culture) to different (different time, different space, different culture). If you arrange the three continuums into a three-dimensional picture you will see the graphic in Figure 4.1. Space is on the X-axis, time is on the Y-axis, and culture is on the Z-axis.

If you were to juxtapose boxes on this 3-D continuum to represent each possible team, there would be eight boxes for eight types of teams. However, because we believe that two of those possibilities (same time, same space, same culture teams and same time, same space, different culture teams) are not really virtual teams that require a distance manager, we will not include them in our discussion. Eliminating these two teams leaves us with six types of virtual teams as represented by the six boxes in Figure 4.2.

Determining What Type of Virtual Team(s) You Have

You can use the questionnaire that follows to determine which virtual teams you use. However, before you answer the questions, a little discussion will be helpful. Assessing time and space differences is pretty straightforward. Team members either share a common space (co-location) or they don't (distributed). They either work the same hours (synchronous) or they don't (asynchronous). But determining whether

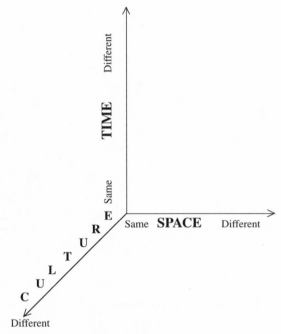

Figure 4.1   Space, Time, and Culture Continuum

they share a common culture (homogeneous) or not (heterogeneous) is more complicated. Ultimately you will need to make a judgement call to use the diagnostic model in this chapter. To help you make this decision, consider these observations:

- A *homogeneous* culture has clearly established norms. These norms (or patterns of behavior) help the people figure out how to communicate, work together, solve problems, and make decisions. Like the autonomic nervous system of the body, norms help facilitate the day-to-day operation of the team without demanding a lot of attention from team members. Typically, a homogeneous culture has clearly understood roles and responsibilities for members, a shared sense of behavior standards, and methods for dealing with nonconformance. Although factors like ethnicity, gender, age, and religious backgrounds affect cultural homogeneity, our experience is that thinking styles may be the most crucial

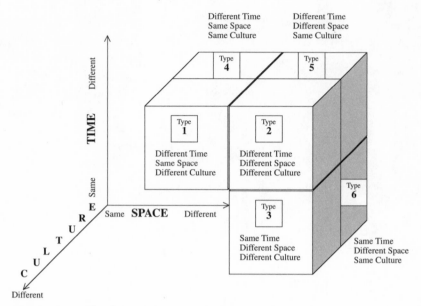

Figure 4.2   Six Types of Virtual Teams

factor of all. Things like life experience, technical or educational background, work experiences, and personal preferences normally affect thinking styles.

- A *heterogeneous* organization (as we define it) is more individualistic in nature. There really isn't a common culture. Norms are not shared. People figure out what to do in each new situation as it arises. One person's perspective on roles and responsibilities and behavior standards may be quite different from that of other people in the organization.

Cautions for Assessing Culture

Two cautions are probably in order here. First, don't assume that a heterogeneous organization is necessarily bad, nor that a homogeneous culture is necessarily good. While it is true that heterogeneous organizations must work harder to accomplish things than effective homogeneous ones, an ineffective homogeneous culture (with strong but dysfunctional norms, for example) may never get out of the starting gates at all. Second, homogeneity doesn't mean that everybody is alike. On the contrary, the most effective homogeneous virtual team cultures we know of are composed of highly diverse people in terms of thinking and life experience who have figured out how to work together effectively. The common problem with homogeneous cultures that have little diversity in membership is that team members get stuck in what experts call *groupthink*—a terminal case of consistency that inhibits creativity and innovation.

The Virtual Team Assessment Questionnaire

Fill in the following questionnaire in order to classify your team(s) into one of the six types of virtual organizations:

Circle One:

1. Do members of the team normally work during the same hours?   Yes   No
2. Do members of the team normally work together at the same place?   Yes   No
3. Do members of the team share a common culture?   Yes   No

If you answered yes to all three questions, or yes to questions 1 and 2, but no to question 3, you are not a distance manager (but thanks for reading the book anyway). For the other possibilities, see Figure 4.3.

Examples of the Six Types of Virtual Teams

Let's consider some common examples for each of the parts of this virtual team typology (see Figure 4.4). An example of a Type 1 team is a customer service team, manufacturing operation, or warehousing team that has multiple shifts operating the same equipment. The only difference between a Type 1 team and a Type 4 team is the degree of homogeneity of the culture. A Type 1 team, for example, might be a service team that answers customer calls about a software product 24 hours a day, in shifts, from the same phone banks. The Type 4 team could be the same operation but it would have a very homogeneous culture as opposed to the heterogeneous culture of the Type 1 team. Unlike the

Instructions: To determine the type of virtual team locate your answers to the three questions on the scoring diagram below:

1. Do members of the team normally work during the same hours?   Yes   No
2. Do members of the team normally work together at the same place?   Yes   No
3. Do members of the team share a common culture?   Yes   No

Question 1	Question 2	Question 3	TEAM TYPE
NO	YES	NO	1
NO	NO	NO	2
YES	NO	NO	3
NO	YES	YES	4
NO	NO	YES	5
YES	NO	YES	6

Figure 4.3   What Kind of Virtual Team Do You Lead?

other teams, Type 1 and 4 teams can communicate by using simple technologies like blackboards and posted charts that are located in a single geography and can be updated by each shift as they leave. To provide some synchronous activities, many of these virtual teams can use shift overlap meetings for face-to-face interaction.

A Type 2 team might be a global project team, large organization, or international product development team. A Type 5 team would be the same, except that it would have a more homogeneous culture. Type 2 and 5 teams are the most difficult to manage because they cross both time and space. Therefore, the teams must become proficient in using asynchronous technologies like e-mail, electronic whiteboards, and voice mail, and in making very good use of limited synchronous time to work with each other using technologies such as teleconferencing and videoconferencing.

A Type 3 team might be a local sales or service team, or a regional consulting firm. A Type 6 team would be the same type of team with a more homogeneous culture. These teams have the benefit of syn-

TYPE	CHARACTER-ISTICS	EXAMPLES	DISTANCE CHALLENGES
1	Different time Same space Different culture	24 hr Teleservice 24 hr Warehouse 24×7 Factory	Cross shift interaction Multicultural interaction
2	Different time Different space Different culture	Global Teams Large Projects Large Organization	Cross time zone interaction Multiple location interaction Multicultural interaction
3	Same time Different space Different culture	Local Sales Team Regional Services	Cross geography interaction Multicultural interaction
4	Different time Same space Same culture	24 hr Teleservice 24 hr Warehouse 24×7 Factory	Cross shift interaction
5	Different time Different space Same culture	Global Teams Large Projects Large Organization	Cross time zone interaction Multiple location interaction
6	Same time Different space Same culture	Local Sales Team Regional Services	Cross geography interaction

Figure 4.4   Examples of Virtual Teams

chronous schedules and can be hooked together electronically in real time through technology. Face-to-face interaction is more difficult, however, as the team members are normally working at different sites.

The first three types of teams (heterogeneous cultures) also require special treatment to create agreements on how to work together. Types 4, 5, and 6 can be maintained with fewer of these interventions if the culture is functional. However, if you have a dysfunctional homogeneous team, the change process often requires extreme measures to modify group norms that have come to be accepted over time.

Most of the remaining book will focus on helping you lead all of these types of virtual teams. But for more specific information about how to make your particular type of team successful read the appropriate following section(s) in this chapter:

Making Type I and Type 4 Teams Successful

Type 1 and Type 4 teams have the advantage of sharing a common space. Use it. Create a physical place that provides a sense of identity and a means for collaboration. Carve out a place for a team room where people can cluster and talk. Sun Microsystems, for example, uses what they call "Sun rooms" as gathering and meeting places. These are small, brightly illuminated rooms that normally have a whiteboard and comfortable chairs (or even a couch in most cases). They are spaces that encourage people to share ideas with each other, solve problems, and collaborate.

Decorate the team space with identity-enhancing graphics. For example, these teams often benefit from posters, charts, and graphs located on the walls. Have team members post their goals, timelines, or other key measures in places where they will be visible to each shift. These types of community report cards can be updated each shift in order to obtain high-quality data, but more important, they are a visible reminder that each shift is part of something that transcends its time period. Post your team charter and operating guidelines on the wall for the same reason. (For more information on how to create these kinds of focusing documents see Chapter 6, "Distance Team Building: Practical Tips for Building Effective Teams," and Chapter 12, "The Necessity of Face-to-Face Meetings.") Some teams create a symbol that they use to reinforce their shared identity with people who work at other times. The Apple Macintosh Design Team posted a pirate flag above their quarters to symbolize their skunk-work operation working on the fringe of the corporation. This flag helped people, regardless of their working hours, to feel part of something bigger than their shift.

The biggest challenge for the Type 1 or Type 4 team, of course, is communicating across the distance of time. Most operations find that they have to create shift overlap in the schedule to accommodate and encourage this communication. This is easier in operations using eight-hour shifts than in organizations using twelve-hour shifts, but it is always preferable to create the opportunity for face-to-face inter-change whenever possible. During the overlap most organizations have some sort of shift download meeting where the incoming team members find out what happened on the last shift. This time is always scarce and should be used efficiently for the activities that are best done face-to-face. If a team decision is to be made, for example, some of the suggestions might first be gathered asynchronously on the team Web site at the convenience of the team members throughout the shifts. The meeting may then be reserved to discuss the pros and cons of each suggestion with all present. Suggestions for other asynchronous communications will be found throughout this book.

The other primary challenge for the Type 1 team that distinguishes it from the Type 4 team is dealing with multiple cultures. See the section on dealing with cultural differences for some tips and traps.

Dealing with Cultural Differences

Cultural differences present a difficult issue that requires some thoughtful investigation on your part. What specifically are the cultural issues? Are they rooted in organizational differences, country-of-origin differences, technical discipline differences, or something else? Treat the situation appropriately. Organizational culture differences, for example, normally require the development of new mutually agreed on operating guidelines for the team. These guidelines are agreements on how to work together that transcend the organizational backgrounds of the team members. They allow people to focus on the here and now instead of on the past. See Chapter 6, "Distance Team Building: Practical Tips for Building Effective Teams," for more information on setting operating guidelines.

Country-of-origin differences and technical discipline differences also benefit from developing these guidelines together as a team. But they normally require more. Sometimes language training is needed to help participants who don't understand the predominant language. Technical training may be required to bridge the chasm caused by technical discipline differences in approaching problems or making decisions. If serious culture differences come from the country of origin (or from issues associated with gender, ethnicity, religion, age, sexual orientation, disability, etc.) then most teams find that they need to receive special training in cross-cultural sensitivity. In some cases professional consultation or mediation may be required. This help is especially important when dealing with issues that may have legal consequences.

Making the Type 2 and Type 5 Teams Successful

The Type 2 and Type 5 teams are the most difficult to lead because they have neither shared time nor shared space as an advantage. Creating an identity and some collaboration, therefore, requires a number of virtual teaming activities and solid use of communication technologies. Type 2 and Type 5 teams are especially vulnerable to a poor start-up. As we have already mentioned, an effective face-to-face start-up is important for any virtual organization. At a minimum, this activity helps people get to know their colleagues, identifies their purpose and key measures, facilitates future collaboration, and clarifies roles and responsibilities. (See Chapter 2, "Five Things That Cripple the Effectiveness of the Distance Manager," Chapter 6, "Distance Team Building," and Chapter 12, "The Necessity of Face-to-Face Meetings," for more information.)

The start-up helps, but it isn't enough. You'll need a way of coordinating the day-to-day work virtually through a variety of conferencing technologies mentioned in more detail later in the book (see all of the chapters in Part III, "The Distance Technology Handbook"). Establish a way to have regular teleconferences and/or videoconferences and/or Web conferences with the team members. These team meetings are necessary to check progress and coordinate. One-on-one virtual meetings between you and each employee may be necessary, but they are insufficient as a coordinating and information-sharing mechanism for Type 2 and Type 5 virtual teams. Team members need to communicate with each other regularly in real time as well. In some cases they may need video. In many cases voice communication or voice communication with shared access to computer files is sufficient. Coordinating the timing of this in a global team can be a headache because someone is almost always required to participate at a bad time for them (e.g., middle of their night, holidays, weekends). Do your best to minimize this problem by choosing times that are least disruptive.

All effective leaders also know that much of the work of a team gets done in informal settings. Co-located team members have a significant advantage. They can run into each other in the hallways, see others during breaks, or meet people at lunch or in the parking lot. This informal interaction not only helps with the socialization needs of team members (people will work and communicate more effectively with people they know than with strangers) but also provides a serendipitous opportunity to coordinate and collaborate ("Hey Jane, I just heard that you're working on the X project; can I ask you a couple of questions?"). Create a virtual water cooler if you don't have a physical one. For example, many teams have a chat room space on their intranet that allows for informal virtual interaction.

In many cases virtual interaction still isn't enough. Effective distance managers strongly recommend that you do something that allows people to discuss things physically as well. The best method for this is a periodic face-to-face meeting. The frequency of these interactions depends on your situation. The leaders we interviewed ranged from never having a face-to-face to having one every other week. The most common frequency is a quarterly meeting that focuses on the things best done in person, including some social activities (e.g., dinner, golf) that facilitate informal interaction. Avoid concerts, movies, or other activities that won't allow people to talk to each other.

Finally, find a way to create virtual team space for Type 2 and Type 5 teams. On some Hewlett-Packard projects, for example, the company actually sets up desks for the off-site team members in the office where most team members are located. This isn't practical or cost-effective in most situations, but where teaming is critical, the company finds that this makes the off-site employees feel more like full partners than periodic associates. At a minimum, set up a team Web site. This will help provide an identity and a shared virtual meeting space for team members. A certain amount of the site should be designed by the team members themselves, to allow them to feel like it is really theirs. Many teams include their photos on the site to personalize the space. Remember that any technology used will require training. Simply assuming that people will figure out how to use the Web site (or e-mail or voice mail, etc.) is a mistake. More on this later.

The other primary challenge for the Type 2 team that distinguishes it from the Type 5 team is dealing with multiple cultures. See the previous section on dealing with cultural differences for some tips and traps.

Making the Type 3 and Type 6 Teams Successful

The advantage of the Type 3 and Type 6 teams is shared time. This allows you to set aside communication and coordination times for virtual interaction with minimal problems. Most of these teams find it useful to have regularly scheduled conference meetings in the same way that co-located teams have staff meetings. The most common frequency for such virtual conferences is weekly, though many of these teams find that a brief daily meeting is helpful to coordinate assignments. (See all of the chapters in Part III, "The Distance Technology Handbook," for more information on using the various communication technologies effectively.)

Type 3 and Type 6 teams are also normally located in a sufficiently small geography so that face-to-face meetings can be held with less expense than for widely distributed teams. It is good practice to schedule these with sufficient frequency that team members can have most of the advantages of a co-located team. For this type of team a quarterly meeting should not be difficult, and an increased frequency is recommended if team members can benefit from sharing ideas, coordinating with others, or joint problem-solving or decision-making activities. Remember to save the face-to-face meetings for things that aren't easily accomplished through virtual interactions. With the possibility of more regular face-to-face meetings in these types of virtual teams than the other types, you might keep a running agenda for the meetings that anyone can contribute to (perhaps a space on your Web site titled "Topics for upcoming face-to-face meetings"). This way, you can schedule more frequent meetings as soon as you have a sufficient agenda to justify one.

The primary difference between a Type 3 and Type 6 team is cultural differences. Type 3 teams benefit from the activities previously mentioned in the section focused on dealing with cultural differences.

Summary

Considering the key virtual team variables of space, time, and culture, we can create a typology of teams that allows us to categorize them into six types. Each type has special, unique challenges. Type 1 and Type 4 teams must find ways to create virtual time. Types 2 and 5 must create virtual time and space. Types 3 and 6 require virtual space. Types 1, 2, and 3 are also challenged with multiple cultures, while Types 4, 5, and 6 have a cohesive culture—a benefit as long as the culture is functional. If it is not, then leadership intervention is required.

Many of the virtual team requirements mentioned in this chapter can be met through real-time and face-to-face activities supplemented with a combination of technologies. Later in the book we will review the technologies for virtual time and space in much greater detail.

References

1. J. P. Donlon, "The Virtual Organization," *Chief Executive (U.S.),* July 1997 n125 p. 58 (8). Reprinted with permission from *Chief Executive.*
2. Jessica Lipnack and Jeffrey Stamps, *Virtual Teams: Reaching Across Space, Time, and Organizations with Technology,* New York: John Wiley & Sons, Inc., 1997. Copyright © 1997 Jessica Lipnack and Jeffrey Stamps. Reprinted by permission of John Wiley & Sons, Inc.
3. Edgar Schein, *Organizational Culture and Leadership* (second edition), Jossey-Bass, January 1997. Copyright © 1997 Jossey-Bass, Inc. Reprinted by permission of John Wiley & Sons, Inc.

Staying Connected and Coordinated: The Dos and Don'ts

The Distance Coach: Getting Peak Performance

Finding good players is easy. Getting them to play as a team is another story.[1]

Major league baseball manager
Casey Stengel

CONTINENTAL AIRLINES INCOMING CEO Gordon Bethune faced a remarkable challenge. According to the U.S. Department of Transportation's customer service surveys, at the time he was tapped to run the company, Continental was one of the worst airlines in America. On-time performance, baggage handling, and customer satisfaction levels were tenth out of the 10 airlines that were ranked. Continental had horrible labor relations, employees hated working there, and in 1994 the company had run out of cash for the third time. They had two bankruptcies, multiple CEOs, terrible labor strikes, and what Bethune thought was a highly questionable strategy ("Be the low-cost airline"). The company had turned into what he called "the largest 'nonprofit' organization in America."[2] Working with a vast workforce whose members often served on virtual teams that were reconfigured for nearly every flight, he was supposed to do a turnaround. But how do you coach a losing team?

The board of directors asked Bethune to put together a plan. He called his solution a "Go Forward" plan, to refocus people on the future instead of the past. In what he calls a "novel concept," Continental decided not to do things that lose money—like providing certain flights that didn't attract enough customers. A review of the income statements showed that the airline was also losing about $6 million a year for being late—half of it going to competitors Delta and American for rebooking customers Continental couldn't serve. Bethune decided to give that $3 million to employees instead of competitors in the form of a bonus for meeting on-time targets. The financial incentive wasn't huge when looked at from an individual employee perspective: It amounted to $65 per person for each month the airline met its targets. But it clearly sent a message to people about what was important in the new Continental.

To facilitate the turnaround, Continental started an intensive communication effort to each employee. Every day information was distributed on the airline's stock price, baggage handling efficiency, on-time performance, and a few other key indicators. Every Friday evening a voice mail from Bethune went out all over the company, reviewing the weekly results and future challenges from the CEO's perspective. Employee newsletters went out to employee homes every month. Every six months there was an open house at headquarters, and Bethune then went to seven major cities to give a presentation that was recorded on videotape and available for traveling employees to take home and watch at their leisure.

Results? By 1998 Continental closed the books for the second consecutive year at $4 billion in cash and equivalents. The company's debt/equity ratio improved from 50 to 1 to 4 to 1. Continental's refurbished fleet is now composed of the newest and fastest airplanes in America and regularly ranks first, second, or third for on-time performance. Remarkably, the airline is now listed as one of *Fortune*'s 100 best companies to work for.[3]

Taking a losing airline team to peak levels of performance required very effective coaching, not only from Bethune but from other leaders as well. We have much to learn about distance coaching from this experience. It is especially impressive in light of the fact that these changes were made with the same employee workforce that had been performing so poorly before. Can good coaching make that much difference? Apparently it can.

Clarify Goals and Measures

What does good coaching entail? How does a distance manager create peak performance? This story illustrates a few keys. Good coaching clarifies goals and measures, and entails lots of communication and employee involvement. The reward systems need to be aligned with the goals.

Goals and measurements are especially important to leaders who must coach from a distance. Metrics are almost like a virtual manager that keeps everyone focused on the most important priorities. They are always there, whether the coach is physically present or not. But as the Continental case illustrates, it takes a lot of effort to determine, communicate, and reinforce performance goals and metrics.

Coaching in virtual organizations consumes a significant amount of the distance leader's time. As virtual employees take on increasingly complex tasks and the decision making and problem solving associated with working remotely, this function becomes an even greater necessity.

Taking a proactive approach to coaching is one way to ease the complexity of distance coaching. Proactive coaching in combination with a technique called Socratic coaching and the use of effective accountability systems can pave the way for mutually satisfying coaching interventions. In this chapter we will examine each of these suggestions in more detail. Additionally, we will discuss what is perhaps the most complicated coaching situation the distance manager faces— identifying and coaching *problem performance.*

Socratic Coaching

Building capability in individuals who are working virtually is one of the most important pieces of coaching a distance manager can do. An effective way to transfer capability is to ask questions instead of giving answers. We call this *Socratic coaching.* The ancient Greek philosopher

Socrates was a great teacher who believed that the most effective way to teach was to ask questions instead of lecturing.

Socratic coaching questions are intended to initiate learning and to help others learn through self-discovery. They are not, however, to be used as an inquisition or "game" such as "20 Questions." The better questions focus on where information can be found or on teaching particular thinking processes that help group members make good decisions. Rather than asking questions that can be answered with a simple "yes" or "no," ask open-ended questions that invite further dialogue and get people thinking. If done well, Socratic coaching teaches, strengthens, and empowers.

Proactive Coaching

Coaching involves more than just addressing performance problems when they occur. It includes coaching up front, along the way, and at the end of projects, assignments, and daily tasks. You can't limit coaching to game time. Good coaches coach before, during, and after the game. The coach who only addresses problems or accomplishments when they arise severely limits his or her ability to affect either the individual or the organization as a whole. You have to coach not just on negative performance, but on positive performance as well.

Being a proactive coach requires learning the skills that are necessary to coach "on the spot." For distance managers, "on-the-spot" coaching usually occurs in a teleconference, videoconference, or when responding to e-mail. Be sensitive to the appropriateness and timing of coaching in those situations. For instance, if the situation calls for corrective feedback, don't provide the coaching during the teleconference while a team member's peers are listening in. Follow-up individually after the call to provide the feedback and to have the coaching discussion.

Bringing a team together at the outset of a project (see Chapter 12, "The Necessity of Face to Face Meetings") is an ideal time to provide up-front coaching. Use Socratic coaching questions (see Figure 5.1 for sample questions) to help team members think through all aspects of the project and its outcome.

Similarly, a wrap-up session at the close of a project or activity provides a good opportunity to reflect on well-dones and opportunities for improvements in future endeavors.

- How will you know if you're successful?
- How will you measure progress?
- What information will you need?
- What are the priorities?
- How will you work with other team members on this?
- What processes/tools will you use?
- Who will give input on the decisions?
- How much will this cost? What will be the impact on the budget?
- How will this affect quality?
- What other alternatives have you considered?
- How can I help?
- What went well in this project/activity?
- What are our key learnings from this project/activity?
- What recommendations would we make for future activities based on this experience?
- What things didn't go as well as we had anticipated? How might we avoid similar problems in the future?

Coaching Questions NOT to Ask
- Yes/No questions (Do you have a plan? Have you used data?)
- Judgment questions (What in heaven's name were you thinking? Why did you do that? Why didn't you check with so and so?)
- Abdication questions (What do you think you should do?)

Figure 5.1   Sample Socratic Coaching Questions

Accountability Systems

More than simple delegation (where managers allocate responsibility only for selected projects or activities), shared accountability creates a feeling of real partnership. Good accountability systems create a feeling of clarity, purpose, and empowerment. They help everyone know who is responsible for what. They also enable people to learn from both their successes and their mistakes.

The keys to accountability are: (1) clarity (What is the area of accountability? Who is responsible for it? Who will help them? How will they help?) and (2) metrics (What are the key measures? Who will track the measures? What will happen when measures are off-target?). Groups that operate effectively in a virtual environment identify the major areas of business accountability for which specific individuals need to be responsible. For example, in a typical project the critical areas of accountability might include customer satisfaction, cost, quality, productivity, and project schedule. See Figure 5.2 for an example of an accountability chart. Some virtual teams display this in the form of a star, with a team member identified as the star point leader for each accountability category.

Once the critical accountability categories are established, performance goals and metrics can be set. These should be: (1) specific; (2) measurable (i.e., based on real business results used throughout the organization); (3) challenging (i.e., difficult enough that people feel motivated to "stretch"); and (4) realistic (i.e., achievable enough that group members feel motivated to make an attempt).

With metrics determined, the team can decide who should be personally accountable for each category. This discussion goes hand-in-hand with the Defining Roles and Responsibilities process outlined in Chapter 6, "Distance Team Building: Practical Tips for Building Effective Teams."

Although the distance manager can never abandon his/her own personal accountability for team results, performance of the entire group improves when individuals accept leadership for key result areas in addition to their normal responsibilities.

Coaching to Improve Performance

Consider the plight of a real distance manager, Joan (not her real name, however), who was the leader of a group of consultants. Even though Joan's team had co-located offices, they were seldom together due to heavy travel and varying work schedules.

About a year after the formation of the team, a new member was hired. Larry (not his real name) was extremely bright, had outstanding academic credentials, and seemed eager to begin his professional career with this as his first job out of graduate school. Initially, things seemed to move along nicely. Larry was a quick learner and immediately assumed responsibility for a couple of major projects, including the relocation of the team's offices. The move went smoothly, in spite of the harried schedules of coworkers, and Larry received effusive public recognition for his contribution and hard work.

Larry's regular responsibilities initially included significant customer phone interface. As part of his development plan, Larry was

Area of Accountability	What are our goals for this area? • Specific • Measurable • Challenging • Realistic	Who is accountable for the area? (Consider individual expertise, immediate needs, and future goals.)	Who has secondary accountability? Who should begin to prepare for future accountability?	What should be expected of all team members to achieve these goals?	What developmental needs are required for the team? For those accountable?
Customer Satisfaction					
Training					
Productivity					
Cost					
Quality					
Scheduling					
Safety					
Other					

Figure 5.2 An Accountability Matrix

asked to serve as customer service manager while he learned the ropes and prepared to move into the role of full-time consultant. The customer service manager role involved scheduling other consultants and helping them prepare materials for presentations.

About six months after Larry was hired, Joan thought she noticed changes in his behavior and performance. About this same time, a client called concerning a scheduling mix-up and mentioned that they had documentation regarding their conversations with Larry, and that it was clearly his error, not theirs. When Joan approached Larry about this and some other scheduling mishaps, he became defensive and blamed the clients and other consultants for the errors. Thinking that she must have caught him on a bad day, Joan urged Larry to watch the scheduling process more closely, and then headed out for another long stretch on the road.

As the weeks progressed, the scheduling problems seemed to subside. As she visited customer sites on consulting assignments, however, she noticed that clients never mentioned Larry—a noticeable departure from his predecessor who clients frequently praised for her helpfulness and cheerful manner.

Unbeknownst to Joan, things were unraveling at warp speed back in the office. When Joan wasn't there, Larry was sullen, unhelpful, and almost uncommunicative with coworkers. He was spending considerable work time on personal interests such as computer games, surfing the net, and writing essays unrelated to work topics—including papers attacking the religious beliefs of a coworker. Joan wasn't in the office, so she had no visibility of this. The few employees who were in the office full-time hesitated to "rat out" another employee, and chose instead to steer clear of Larry as much as possible.

Finally, Joan had a break in her travel schedule and was able to be in the office for several weeks. It was during this time that she experienced Larry's change in behavior firsthand. Although he was pleasant enough to her, she noticed he was much less so with others—especially those who he considered to be lower in the hierarchy than he was.

Joan quickly set up a one-on-one coaching session with Larry to discuss her observations. It didn't go well. Larry blew up, Joan lost her cool, and for days following there was considerable tension in the office. Joan determined that she would have to terminate Larry and began working on a corrective action plan. Somewhat to her relief, however, before she had a chance to present the plan to Larry he gave his notice and left two weeks later, just 15 months after he started with the company.

"What went wrong?" Joan wondered. "How could this have spiraled out of control like this?" "And how can I avoid it in the future? My travel schedule is just going to get worse! I can't possibly coach and travel at the same time! I just want to give up on this management stuff!"

Joan certainly isn't alone. In fact, the majority of distance leaders have an even more difficult situation. Whereas Joan shared a home base with the people she managed, many distance managers do not. As we have concluded in other chapters in this book, many are separated from team members by thousands of miles and may see them only occasionally, if at all. So how does the distance leader stay on top of the coaching process? How does he/she get the kind of information that will allow him/her to coach appropriately and in a timely manner? A few tips can help.

Tips for Distance Coaching

Tip Number 1. Respond to subtleties and nuances. Leading across miles demands constant vigilance on the part of the leader to watch for clues that will tell him or her when to step in and coach. In Joan's case, for instance, the combination of Larry's reaction to her initial coaching coupled with the difference in client response to Larry versus his predecessor could have alerted her to intervene further.

Without singling out Larry, she could have solicited feedback from clients regarding their satisfaction with her organization's customer service. What she learned after Larry's departure was that several clients had been adversely impacted by Larry's behavior. While none of them had felt it was their place to intervene earlier, they did raise the issue once they knew Larry was gone. Had Joan asked for their feedback sooner, it might have opened the door for them to provide helpful observations and to surface problems they were encountering. This would then have allowed Joan the opportunity to coach Larry much earlier.

Learning from her experience with Larry, Joan later had a very different coaching experience. When she first noticed some early indicators of potential problems with a different employee, Joan sat down and had a coaching conversation with her about performance concerns. In this case early intervention produced a very positive response. The employee improved her behavior before it could become a difficult-to-change habit, and she actually thanked Joan for her quick response. "I appreciate you letting me know about these things and helping me to become more successful," said the employee after the feedback session.

Tip Number 2. Implement a peer feedback process. Managing from a distance severely limits a leader's visibility of performance. Even if they aren't co-located, peers often work together on projects and understand the demands, requirements, and expected outcomes facing one another. If properly prepared, peers can provide very helpful coaching to each other. However, unless a formal system for doing so is provided and giving feedback is an established norm within the group, peers are often reluctant to raise issues regarding one another's performance.

One useful tool for peer feedback is the *Stop, Start, Continue* exercise. This process can be used at regular intervals (e.g., every six months, once a year) as a way for every member of the group to receive feedback from every other member on what they do that is helpful to others, what is not helpful, and ideas for how they can improve in the future (see Figure 5.3 for a sample "Stop, Start, Continue" worksheet). The process is most effective when the feedback is delivered via a one-on-one conversation conducted face-to-face or over videoconference.

In the case of Joan and Larry, if regular peer feedback sessions had

Stop	**Start**	**Continue**
• Sending me non-work-related e-mail (jokes and stories).	• Telling me openly and honestly when you disagree with me.	• Your excellent technical work.
• Interrupting me during discussions.	• Taking more credit for your ideas.	• Your honest, caring feedback.
		• Involving me with you in solving problems that affect both of us.

Figure 5.3 Stop, Start, Continue Example

been a part of the culture, Larry would have had the chance to receive more timely feedback than Joan was able to provide. Further, Larry would have had the advantage of multiple points of view, thus reinforcing Joan's observations and those of the clients. Some virtual team members will complain that their manager isn't around enough to understand the issues and problems facing the team. Having peers give input provides a more balanced and accurate picture.

Tip Number 3. Establish regular one-on-one coaching sessions with each employee. Mark Nyman, Director of Business Transformation at MediaOne and formerly an internal OD consultant with Altura Energy, has had numerous opportunities to work with virtual teams and to consult with distance managers. He counsels distance leaders to find ways to stay in touch with team members. "You can't assume everything is OK," cautions Nyman. "The need to stay in touch and in tune is critical. Some leaders assume that if you don't hear anything, that it is fine—'No news is good news.' Some individuals will use the fact that they are in a virtual situation as an excuse not to be structured about staying in touch with the team. But the leaders who are effective are the ones who are out there a lot."

Regular one-on-one discussions are an effective way to do what Nyman is suggesting. Such sessions allow the leader to stay up-to-date on projects, keep informed on issues and problems, and strengthen and maintain good relationships with employees. Having such sessions on a regular basis moves the coaching process into the arena of developmental conversations, versus coaching only when problems arise. Some leaders choose to follow a standard format for these discussions. See Figure 5.4 for a sample of such a format.

One can only speculate that had Joan initiated and followed through with regularly scheduled one-on-one discussions, perhaps Larry wouldn't have responded so negatively during their first conversation. If a manager only calls or shows up when there is trouble, employees begin to believe that "no news is good news" and may feel immediately defensive when asked to meet with the leader.

Tip Number 4. Use a structured improvement plan. When performance issues warrant it, request that the employee put together a performance improvement plan that he/she will commit to. Be clear about expectations and set boundaries for what needs to be included in the plan, but keep responsibility for success with the individual. Finally,

---

Team member name: Date:

1. Update on personal development plan:

2. Discussion of key projects (including deadlines, issues, problems, etc.):

3. Business information for team member:

4. Feedback on team member performance (including well dones, areas for improvement, etc.):

Figure 5.4   One-on-One Coaching Format

provide regular coaching and other help as needed to help ensure a successful outcome.

Summary

Good performance coaching is the hallmark of an effective leader. Coaching proactively is most effective and includes coaching at various points of a project or activity. Socratic coaching allows the individual to learn from the leader. Establishing clear accountability systems aids both the coach and the team members in successfully carrying out responsibilities and assuring that nothing slips between the cracks. Having clear goals and measures identifies the target.

When coaching to improve performance, the following four steps can be especially helpful: Be vigilant about watching for subtle clues and then taking action on them. Implement a peer feedback process that allows individuals to obtain a broader, more well-rounded perspective on their performance. Establish regular one-on-one sessions as a matter of course with every employee. This allows the distance manager to build better rapport with team members and sets an expectation that performance discussions are intended to help the individual be successful. And finally, when performance issues call for it, have the individual take responsibility to create an improvement plan. Then coach him/her to help ensure long-term success.

References

1. Novasoft Quotationary™ CD, 1999.
2. Sheila Puffer, "Continental Airlines' CEO Gordon Bethune on Teams and New-Product Development," *The Academy of Management Executive*, August 1999 v13 i3 p. 28.
3. Ibid.

Distance Team Building: Practical Tips for Building Effective Teams

Working virtually requires the team leader or manager to give equal time and attention to team dynamics and task accomplishment. In other words, balancing task and process.

Curt Crosby, Senior Quality Consultant
Sun Microsystems

LOUISE (NOT HER real name) is a human resources manager in the West Coast office of a fast-growing high-tech company headquartered on the East Coast. Almost immediately after Louise was hired she was assigned to be part of a virtual team charged with ensuring a fast and effective start-up of the West Coast office. Members of the start-up team were located across four states, six cities and three time zones. Every member of the team was bright, highly skilled, and hardworking, almost to a fault. To their credit, the West Coast start-up was flawless—

almost. As Louise talks about her experience on this team, it is clear that there is unmistakable pride in the final outcome, but that the process to get there left significant unpleasant residue.

Louise can list all the reasons the West Coast start-up team was successful—they had clear roles and responsibilities, established regular means of communication, developed a workable and aggressive action plan, and held weekly teleconferences to ensure that the project and key assignments were on track. So what was missing? What left team members with such an unpleasant taste in their mouth and reservations about participating on future projects of this kind?

As Louise can attest, a few key steps were missed. For instance, the team members never met face-to-face. While that isn't always a show-stopper for building a strong team, it made considerable difference in this case. The team leader, in an earnest attempt to make sure the project stayed on track, chose to focus only on getting the business at hand completed. She never took time to address the social aspects of the team dynamics. As Louise will verify, each meeting became a painful, almost humiliating experience as each member was asked to report on his/her assignments and then take feedback from other team members. "This was extremely painful—to take criticism from people we had never met and had no relationship with. Then, to make matters worse, the team leader would berate team members in front of one another— again without first establishing any kind of relationship between her and them or between team members. I don't mind feedback at all if I have at least met the other person or had some kind of opportunity to establish a relationship with him or her. But we never met one another until well after the project was completed. I doubt that many of us would sign on to do another project with that team leader."

As Louise's story illustrates, another primary challenge of the distance manager is building cohesion in a team separated by time, space, and culture. Although more difficult to do in virtual teams than in those that are co-located and share common time and culture, there are some things that can help in this endeavor.

In this chapter we will explore techniques and tools employed by successful virtual teams to strengthen their members' ability to work together effectively. We will examine two kinds of approaches to building effective teams. One consists of team-building activities a team can experience in which they accomplish a task and have a tangible output when they are done. This will include such things as creating a team charter, setting operating guidelines, and defining team member roles and responsibilities. The second group of tips involves things the team leader can do to help the team coalesce. This includes techniques such as providing good team facilitation, establishing boundary conditions, modeling and teaching conflict management skills, teaching effective decision-making processes, and integrating members who are new to the team.

Team-Building Activities with Tangible Outcomes

Tip Number 1. Create a team charter. A charter provides a sense of purpose for the team and a clear definition of the team's role. Not only does the charter itself provide direction, the process of creating it is a team-building activity. The charter discussion allows each team member to express his or her views on what the team's core purpose and objectives are, thus clarifying early on where time and energy will be focused.

Additionally, a well-defined charter will provide a basis for setting goals and making decisions. Once the team members are clear on their overarching purpose, they can establish goals and timelines to assure that they achieve it. This in turn will serve to minimize unproductive conflict within the team, give individuals a sense of purpose, and allow the distance manager to provide appropriate coaching and feedback along the way. See Figures 6.1 and 6.2 for examples of virtual team charters.

Tip Number 2. Set operating guidelines. Another team-building activity that creates a useful by-product is establishing operating guidelines

---

Charter

- The purpose of the Artex sales team is to provide high quality, timely service to all Artex customers.
- Our primary responsibilities are to respond to service requests within 4 hours and to complete internal paperwork within 36 hours of service.
- Our top priority is to meet or exceed customer expectations.

Figure 6.1   A Simple Field Service Team Example of a Team Charter

---

Charter of the 2002 Drive Shaft Design Team

The purpose of the 2002 Drive Shaft Design Team is to identify design and safety improvements for drive shafts on the B and D series for 2002 models of Fiat, Daewoo, and Volvo.

The key results expected from the DSD Team are:

1. Deliver new alpha level designs by 11/30/01.

2. Operate within established budget.

3. Incorporate customer input acquired at the September 2001 customer design conference.

4. Obtain final customer design approvals by 2/1/02.

Figure 6.2 A Sample Charter of a Product Design Team

together. Operating guidelines are agreements for group interaction which are developed and supported by all team members. Their purpose is to shape group interaction and to help group members understand what is acceptable behavior within a group. A good set of operating guidelines provides direction for such activities as making decisions, solving problems, providing leadership, and conducting meetings. See Figures 6.3 and 6.4 for examples of virtual team operating guidelines.

In an interview in *Getting Results,* Jacklyn Kostner discusses what she calls an *alignment tool,* which serves the same purpose as operating guidelines or group norms. She explains that "while the company's vision or mission statement tells employees what needs to be achieved, the alignment tool tells them how to do it." She describes the alignment tool created by one company that outlined what was needed to provide outstanding customer service. "The list included everything from answering the phone within three rings to never rejecting unusual customer requests. It was the alignment tool—and it helped the company double its market share."[1]

If the team does not deliberately set operating guidelines, then the team's norms or habits become the guidelines by default. This can be especially problematic when norms converge from different geographic, ethnic, or organization cultures. Taking time as soon as possible after the formation of a team to facilitate the development of guidelines will help not only the team members be more effective, but

---

Operating Guidelines

- We answer customer calls within 24 hours, and within 2 hours if we are in the office.
- If we have a concern about a team member, we express it to him/her directly, not talk about them to other team members.
- We call the office at least once a day.
- We follow-through on everything we commit to do.
- We listen to others when they are talking. We don't hold sidebar conversations during meetings.
- If we have a conflict with another team member, we respectfully describe our concern and work to jointly resolve the issue.
- We share client discussions with other team members.

Figure 6.3   Operating Guidelines for a Team of Consultants

will also ease the way for the manager. The more the team members are equipped to self-manage their day-to-day interactions, the freer the manager is to focus on strategic issues that concern the team.

Tip Number 3. Clearly define team member roles and responsibilities. It's no secret that one of the major causes of any team (virtual or otherwise) breakdown is lack of clear roles and responsibilities. When

---

Operating Guidelines

- We rotate the times of our meetings so that we minimize negative impact on any one team member.
- We complete all assignments on time or let the team know at least two weeks ahead if a deadline must be missed.
- We respect cultural holidays and customs of all team members.
- We will use French as the language of communication, both written and verbal.
- We keep all information shared by team members confidential. This is especially critical as we are representing different, sometimes competing corporations.
- We notify the team in advance if we cannot attend a scheduled meeting.

Figure 6.4   Operating Guidelines for a Multicultural, Cross-Organizational New-Product Development Team

roles are not clearly defined, well-intentioned team members, in an effort to move a project along, may find themselves tripping over one another or failing to meet deadlines or other expectations. The team manager can prevent this kind of dysfunction by leading the team through a discussion in which each team member's role is clarified and agreed to by the entire team.

A good way to start the discussion is to begin by jointly articulating what should be expected of *all* team members. Once in agreement on common areas of responsibility, move on to determining individual roles. A clear understanding of each individual's expected contribution will allow team members to integrate what they do with the efforts of their associates.

Many teams also find it useful to identify the degree to which members need to learn one another's roles for backup or development. If it is determined that cross-training or multiskilling is required, well-thought-out plans for achieving this must be agreed to. Will the cross-training require that the team members meet face-to-face, or can some of the training be done over the intranet or Internet? What are acceptable deadlines for the training to take place? What is the required budget for making this happen? Are any other resources needed?

Leadership Tips for Building Effective Teams

Now we'll consider some general advice for creating effective teams. Although not all of the following tips are specific team-building activities, they are all necessary for building an effective one:

Tip Number 4. Provide both task and process team facilitation. Team members often tend to focus heavily on the technical or task aspects of the work—sometimes at the expense of the social or process side. Richard Thier at Xerox Corporation explains how important the balanced facilitation of a virtual team is: "The effective leaders I have worked with facilitated involvement. They were able to surface the personal dimensions of members." Thier goes on to explain that by facilitating the development of the personal dimension of the team's composition, these leaders helped team members build camaraderie. This in turn aided them in working together during crises or particularly difficult junctures in projects.

When working virtually, a distinct effort is required to build the social structure of the team. Create virtual water coolers or virtual hallways where informal pleasantries and office banter can occur. This might be done at the beginning or end of teleconferences or video/satellite meetings. Some teams engage in mini-team-building activities by having everyone e-mail a description of one of their hobbies before the meeting. The facilitator reads the descriptions and then people try to match the team members with their hobbies. Another example is to have each person describe one of their heroes and explain why that individual affected them so strongly. A further example might be to ask everyone to describe their favorite previous job and explain why they liked it so much.

These kinds of activities can help team members get to know more about each other at a personal level. With this type of facilitated activity the quality of team interaction and trust tends to improve. However, be careful to choose an activity that is acceptable to all cultures represented on the team. Activities that are perfectly acceptable to Americans or Australians, for example, may require a level of disclosure that is very uncomfortable for Japanese or Vietnamese team members. What someone with a production background might find acceptable could be inappropriate for someone with an engineering background, and so forth. While some kind of visual or verbal contact is most effective, some of the social connection can also be carried out via e-mail.

Tip Number 5. Use boundary conditions. In traditional organizations, managers often have been expected to control all aspects of the work that is being performed by their direct reports. Since management had "rightful" control over the way work was performed, it followed that all alterations were issued by management in the form of orders, commands, or directives. When managing virtual teams, this clearly is not possible.

A directive attempts to specify what needs to be done and how it should be accomplished, whereas a boundary condition addresses only what the constraints or limitations are and leaves the determination of what and how work gets done up to the team. See Figure 6.5. Boundary conditions help focus the group without unduly constraining its members. In a virtual world where team members and their manager are separated in time and space, having the flexibility to take action within known constraints is crucial to team success.

Directives	Boundary Conditions
Specifies what needs to be done and how it should be accomplished	Specifies the constraints and limitations that must be considered before the group determines what is to be done and how it can be accomplished
Management driven	Shared leadership

Figure 6.5   Directives Versus Boundary Conditions
Adapted from the Leadership Skills training program, The Fisher Group, Inc. © 1999. All rights reserved. Used with permission.

Tip Number 6. Teach and model how to give and receive feedback. An important part of working successfully as a team is knowing how to both give and receive feedback. Working in an environment that fosters feedback allows individuals to flourish and grow as they strive to continuously learn and improve their performance. Giving feedback is seldom comfortable in any setting—how many of us were told as kids that "if we can't say anything nice, don't say anything at all"? When compounded with cross-cultural issues the process becomes even more complex.

As a virtual team leader, first learn about what feedback protocols are appropriate for the various cultures represented on your team. Then coach accordingly.

Consider the following reminders about effective feedback:

- Always strive to maintain the self-esteem of the individual. The intent of sharing feedback is to help the team and its members be successful, not to simply get something "off your chest."
- Do not "stockpile" feedback. Provide the feedback as soon after the situation as possible.
- Carefully select the timing and location for delivering the feedback. When giving feedback that is intended to correct or develop a team member, it should be done in private. This both protects the individual's self-esteem and maintains the confidentiality of the situation.
- Before sitting down to give feedback, consider practicing with a colleague or someone else who isn't close to the situation. Hear-

ing yourself talk helps you to select useful phrases or comments and to eliminate words or statements that may damage the relationship or the effectiveness of the feedback.

Feedback is, of course, a two-way process. Receiving feedback is as critical a skill as being able to deliver it. A few ideas to keep in mind when receiving feedback include:

- Others may see areas for improvement in us that we don't see in ourselves. Therefore, it is wise to be open to the insights and suggestions of others.
- Most people offer feedback because they care about our success and the success of the team or project.

Tip Number 7. Teach and model good conflict-management skills. In virtual teams, as in any other kind of team, conflict, if managed well, can be a source of strength and creativity. Conflict defines. It forces the individuals or the team involved to examine their assumptions, ideas, and solutions.

However, if left unmanaged or unresolved, conflict can become destructive, eroding team members' confidence and trust in one another. When setting operating guidelines, it is sometimes a good idea to incorporate a statement or two about how conflict will initially be handled and what to do when the parties involved cannot reach a resolution (e.g., do they bring in a manager or other third party to facilitate?).

A defined process for resolving conflict can be useful. The five steps in Figure 6.6 provide such a process.

Tip Number 8. Employ empathic listening skills. A large part of establishing rapport and trust with others has to do with listening to them in a way that allows you to fully understand both the content and the emotions associated with their message. Building a team effectively requires developing these skills. In virtual teams they are especially critical, because empathic listening is not only much more important but also more difficult to do when you are not face-to-face.

Empathic listening means that you listen to understand and to empathize. One clear method of checking for understanding involves repeating what the other person said, *to their satisfaction.* This can be especially helpful for the leader communicating across geographic and

Step 1: Acknowledge that there is conflict and together define what it is.
Step 2: Put the conflict in perspective with the overall purpose and goals of the team.
Step 3: Provide everyone the opportunity to voice their point of view.
Step 4: Ask questions to clarify needs, expectations, and overall understanding of the issue(s).
Step 5: Jointly develop an action plan.

Figure 6.6   Steps to Resolving Conflict
Adapted from the Leadership Skills training program, The Fisher Group, Inc. © 1999. All rights reserved. Used with permission.

cultural lines. Once the other individual agrees that you have accurately heard them, you can move on to communicate your own points.

Demonstrating empathy (e.g., "I think I understand why you feel that way," or, "If I were in your position I'd probably feel the same") can help the other person feel that he or she has been heard and understood. You can demonstrate empathy for a position whether you agree with it or not.

Finally, avoiding defensiveness is critical to maintaining a positive and productive tone in the conversation. If the leader can model the expression and acceptance of forthright and honest opinions, the result is likely to be clearer understanding, better-quality decisions, and improved relationships on which to build future discussions.

Tip Number 9. Develop good decision-making processes. As in any kind of team, people in virtual teams need to learn different methods of decision making and clearly understand their role in that process. Perhaps most important, they need to learn to reach consensus on key decisions. Building consensus is a key to building the trust, participation, and competence that sustain well-functioning teams. Consensus should not be confused with *unanimity.* Figure 6.7 describes the difference between a consensus and a unanimous decision. Discussing various approaches to decision making and when each might be appropriate in this team can eliminate some of the confusion and frustration often associated with making team decisions over time and space. Knowing when to use which method will also lead to better-quality decisions.

Tip Number 10. Integrate new team members effectively. Karen Petty, a human resources manager in the Federal Way, Washington,

Consensus	*Unanimous*
• Does not necessarily mean that every member of the group thinks the best possible decision has been made. • No one is morally, ethically, or professionally violated by the decision. • Every member of the group will actively support the decision.	• Everyone agrees that the best possible decision has been made.

Figure 6.7   Consensus Versus Unanimous Decision Making
Adapted from the Team Resource Skills training program, The Fisher Group, Inc. © 2000. All rights reserved. Used with permission.

office of Capital One, speaks of a virtual team leader who made it a point to call each new member personally to welcome them to the team. Rather than just e-mailing or leaving a voice mail for them to let them know about the upcoming meeting, this leader took the time to bring each new member up to speed on the team's history, progress to date, processes and procedures, other team members, individual roles and responsibilities, and so forth. She then took time in the next teleconference or video meeting to introduce the new member and give him or her an opportunity to virtually meet all of the other members. As Karen explains, "It was a nice recognition of the person rather than just the task or the team's assignment."

Other steps to include in orienting a new team member include:

- Clarify the purpose, priorities, and parameters or boundaries of the team.
- Clarify the team member's specific role and responsibilities.
- Introduce the new team member to the team's customers and/or suppliers.
- Review the team's operating guidelines and ask the new member if he or she can support them.
- Review teleconference and videoconference protocols and etiquette.

- Review team protocols for e-mail or other communication.
- Review key timelines and describe the team's process for reviewing progress against the timelines.

Summary

There are numerous tools and techniques to help a team work together effectively. Those that include a team-building activity that produces tangible results include creating a team charter, setting operating guidelines, and defining team member roles and responsibilities. Actions the team leader can take to help the team bond and work together effectively include providing team facilitation, clarifying boundary conditions, teaching and modeling good feedback and conflict management skills, employing empathic listening skills, helping the team develop good decision-making processes, and integrating new team members effectively.

While there is no one approach or technique that will ensure a smooth ride for virtual teams, these eight points can help you avoid many of the more serious pitfalls that often plague virtual teams. An effective virtual team leader will give equal attention to both process and task, thus helping ensure an outcome that is successful and sustainable.

Reference

1. Jacklyn Kostner, in "Learn to be a Distance Manager," (based on an interview with Richard Lally) in *Getting Results,* July 1997 v 42 n7 p. 6.

7

Distance Training: Building Skills in Remote Sites

For Web meetings to work you need to simulate a face-to-face environment as much as possible. In training sessions, for example, you have to find out if people understand what you're talking about. In a face-to-face meeting you can look at body language to figure that out. In a virtual setting you can't. So you have to ask them every once in a while. I often use polling. I'll preprogram a question into the presentation that says something like, "Does this make sense to you?" and ask them all to respond either "yes" or "no." When I get the poll back I know whether I have to adapt or not.

Peter Bartlett, Program Manager
Hewlett Packard

Not long after receiving a certification from an outside training vendor to teach one of their leadership training programs, Lynn Buchanan, a training manager at Weyerhaeuser Company, was faced with the dilemma of how to distribute the training across multiple sites. The vendor's materials were initially written for classroom presentation and included numerous interactive exercises.

After pondering for some time how to deliver the training, Lynn decided to adapt the materials for remote training. First she taught the participants at the remote sites how to use their internal virtual meeting process (Microsoft Netmeeting™). She set up her materials, including a computer with the training slides on it, a computer projector for on-site participants, and a telephone to connect with remote sites, in a classroom at Weyerhaeuser corporate headquarters in Federal Way, Washington. Some of the class members attended the session in the room with Lynn, while others hooked in via computers, telephones, and headsets from their offices in other states.

On their computers each of the remote attendees could view the images Lynn was using for the lecture portions of the training, and they could hear her lecture via the headsets and telephone linkup. (The off-site participants used headsets instead of speakerphones to eliminate distractions for those in cubicle offices around them.)

For the interactive portions of the training such as small-group case studies, brainstorming sessions, one-on-one discussions and so forth, Lynn grouped each of the remote employees with one of the small groups in the classroom. She had one of the remote participants facilitate and capture the discussion notes on the computer during the small-group discussion to ensure that they stayed engaged. As the remote participant captured the notes, the whole class could see them either on their own or on the classroom computer.

When this first experimental training session was completed, Lynn asked the group for feedback. The response was unanimous—everyone agreed that the session had worked surprisingly well. Those in remote sites stated that it was 90 percent as good as being in the same room and that the 10 percent they sacrificed was worth not having to travel or be away from home and family. Money saved on travel costs was an additional benefit during a time of scaled-back budgets.

By the time this book is published, this "experiment" will probably sound archaic. Technology is advancing at such a fast pace and in such exciting ways that remote training is fast becoming the delivery method of choice for all kinds of topics. This is good news for distance leaders who struggle with the challenge of how to provide skill-building and learning activities for a team that is distributed across time, space, and culture.

And for those concerned that Web-based delivery isn't as effective as the traditional classroom environment, consider this: There is actually historical evidence and research to support the notion that training doesn't have to be done in classic classroom style to be effective. According to one of the earliest studies on media-comparison for training, multiple training media compared favorably to classroom training. In the research study, the same material was put in film, in a classroom training session, and in a self-study handbook. There was no significant difference in learning between the three groups studied. Hundreds of later studies have verified these conclusions. Effective distance learning courses are available in virtually every major university in the world now. It is the design of the instruction that causes learning—not whether it is delivered in person or through another medium, such as the Web.[1]

However, in spite of such encouraging data, there is no doubt that Web-based training does present its own set of challenges. In this chapter we will share tips to ensure that Web-based training is successful, so that those using it can reap the benefits it provides.

Web Training Tips

Tip Number 1. Limit Web-based training sessions to two hours or less. Working virtually via technologies such as computers, videoconferencing, and teleconferencing is extremely tiring. Two hours is the maximum span that almost anyone can be effective working remotely.

Tip Number 2. Where possible, use a combination of remote training and face-to-face sessions. Even if people aren't "technophobic," some topics or discussions are still more effective face-to-face. Adult learners have "an enduring preference for face-to-face, real-time, interactive learning environments."[2] As Margaret Driscoll points out in her critically acclaimed book, *Web-based Training: Using Technology to Design Adult Learning Experiences,* "Adult learners also bring a wealth of real-life experience to training that can be a resource for learning."[3] Driscoll suggests that when using Web-based training the trainers "create interactions in which learners share their experiences with others."[4] As Buchanan discovered in her leadership training class, much of this can be done remotely. However, adding some face-to-face time enhances the training dramatically.

Tip Number 3. Stay focused on *results,* not *activities.* In other words, don't do training for training's sake. Make sure the training provided is linked to organization goals or the professional development goals of participants. This is good advice regardless of the methodology being used to train.

Tip Number 4. Take into consideration the environment in which the individual(s) will be located. For instance, if you are expecting remote participants to log on and train from a home office, make sure they will have the privacy, quiet, and uninterrupted time necessary to allow them to fully engage and participate. This is probably resolved or thwarted by good planning—letting each individual know what the process will be, how long it will take, and what preparations need to be undertaken to ensure that learning can occur.

Tip Number 5. Assess the needs of your team to assure that the appropriate topics and methods of delivery are used. Remember that different people learn in different ways. Most people have preferred learning styles. One of the authors of this book, for example, is an auditory-dominant learner. While Web-based training activities supplemented by simultaneous teleconferencing are very effective for this person, Web training modules without sound are not very effective. The other author is a visual-dominant learner. High-impact graphics (especially with video) are more helpful to this author than to the other one.

Know how your team members respond to training and plan accordingly. To reach the broadest possible audience, choose training options that appeal to a variety of the senses (and learning styles) and have a high degree of interactivity.

Tip Number 6. Try to simulate face-to-face training as much as possible. As the quote that opens this chapter suggests, simulating a face-to-face training environment is very helpful. In synchronous training use *polling.* Polling is a process of asking participants to periodically respond to questions during a presentation to keep them involved and engaged. It also allows the trainer to slow down, speed up, or make other appropriate modifications that a trainer who was physically present would notice (maybe without even asking) by looking at the participants. Do other things that simulate the physical environment as well. Asking people to break away from their computers and do an assignment with the other people in their location is helpful. For asynchronous training have people e-mail an instructor with questions that will be responded to shortly—thereby allowing team members to approximate face to face interaction.

Tip Number 7. Carefully select the method of Web-based training. Depending on the topic, Web-based training can be delivered any number of ways. For example, self-paced learning (one person sitting in front of a computer operating the training at the speed that is right for him or her) is very useful for technical skill development. Using video is also helpful in this regard. Instead of saying, "Here is how you do a search on the Internet," for example, incorporate a video of someone going through the process step by step, allowing the learner to stop the program and repeat sections that he or she didn't understand.

However, self-paced training is not as useful for social skill development that requires interaction with others. Developing social skills such as giving and receiving feedback, resolving conflict, and communicating effectively require practice sessions with other people. These types of training activities are better suited to either face-to-face activities or to instructor-led Web-based presentations that a whole team participates in at the same time, even if they are located in different places (as illustrated by the case that opens this chapter).

Summary

Continuous improvement, at both the organization and the individual level, is a prerequisite for success in any organization today. This requires that the distance manager be vigilant about ensuring that ongoing training is available for those in their organization. While technology has opened many doors to remote learning, it is not without its challenges. For instance, the taxing nature of training methods that utilize technologies such as computers, videoconferencing, or teleconferencing, requires that such sessions be limited to no more than two hours.

Remote training also necessitates that participants be well prepared in advance so that they can allot the required time or make any necessary accommodations to ensure they are undisturbed and can give the session their full attention.

Distance learning is still an evolving process. It's a good idea, therefore, to include some face-to-face time as part of remote training where possible. Doing so helps meet the unique needs of adult learners. Also, using techniques such as polling can help to simulate the physical environment, bridge the distance gap, and provide a greater sense of community learning.

Finally, all training, remote or otherwise, needs to be focused on achieving results. This requires that the distance manager carefully assess the needs of his or her team and then select appropriate topics and methods of delivery to meet those needs. Selecting the right approach for Web-based training (e.g., self-paced training versus an instructor-led Web-based group presentation) should be based on the topic (i.e., technical skill versus social skill development).

Careful attention to the unique challenges associated with remote learning, coupled with good planning, can help ensure that maximum benefit is derived from this important investment of time and money.

References

1. Ruth Colvin Clark and Chopeta Lyons, "Using Web-based Training Wisely," *Training,* (July 1999), p. 51. Reprinted with permission from the July 1999 issue of *Training* magazine. Copyright 1999. Bill Communications, Minneapolis, Minnesota. All rights reserved. Not for resale.
2. Ibid.
3. Margaret Driscoll, *Web-based Training: Using Technology to Design Adult Learning Experiences,* San Francisco:Jossey-Bass/Pfeiffer, 1998, p. 14. Reprinted by permission of Jossey-Bass, Inc., a subsidiary of John Wiley & Sons, Inc. © 1998 Jossey-Bass/Pfeiffer.
4. Ibid.

8

Building Trust from a Distance

Instead of evolving slowly through stages, trust in virtual teams tends to be established—or not—right at the outset. The first interactions of the team members are crucial.[1]

Sifkka L. Jarvenpaa, Professor and Researcher
University of Texas at Austin

T HE EXTRAORDINARY PERFORMER gives full effort regardless of whether the boss is watching. He or she is self-motivated, worries about work issues whether or not he or she is "on-the-clock," and is perpetually trying to improve work processes and relationships. Why do people offer discretionary effort? Ask yourself why you do. Many people report that they give special effort only when they feel trusted and supported, and conversely, when they trust and respect their leader. Rare are the employees who excel under the punitive thumb of someone they don't trust and who they feel does not trust them. At a minimum, without trust, productivity suffers as team members play politics, spend time covering themselves and being compliant to dictates that they know are counterproductive, instead of working on real work issues that affect customers.

In this chapter we will examine several key actions that can build or erode trust when working virtually. We will discuss specific actions the leader can take to create the kind of environment where team members who may rarely see one another or the leader will want to give that discretionary effort that separates a good team from a great one. Some of these tips focus primarily on building trust between the leader and the team. Others suggest ways to build trust between team members.

Tips for Developing Trust

Tip Number 1. Communicate openly and frequently. When Continental's Bethune was charged with the Herculean task of rebuilding trust in the airline besieged by labor strife, one thing he did that helped significantly was to initiate open and frequent communication. Review Chapter 5, "The Distance Coach: Getting Peak Performance," for more information on how he used weekly voice mail, monthly newsletters, and semiannual videotaped presentations to communicate with every Continental employee.

Don't make distance workers guess what you're thinking. Tell them. Unfortunately, distance employees tend to believe that no news is bad news. A lack of interaction across distance erodes trust.

Try to use methods that make communications feel more like a face-to-face interaction. Richard Thier, an organization effectiveness manager at Xerox, suggests imbedding pictures of team members into computer technology so that when communicating on the intranet team members can "see" each other and you. In Thier's experience, this helps to create social bonding and to eliminate at least one of the barriers to building trust that many teams encounter—not seeing one another face-to-face.

Tip Number 2. To get trust, give trust. The best way to create an environment of trust is to begin by trusting others. Leaders set the example. Waiting to give trust to employees until they earn it is never as effective as assuming they are trustworthy unless they prove otherwise. As team members come to feel that you trust them, they will find it easier to trust you.

Tip Number 3. Be honest. This is perhaps the single most important variable that affects trust. Leaders who demonstrate openness about their actions, intentions, and vision soon find that people respond positively to self-disclosure and sincerity. Share good news and bad news openly. An open and honest business climate is likely to eliminate company gossip, diffuse inappropriate politics, and stifle corporate intrigue. Further, great leaders know that they are not perfect; they make mistakes. What do they do when that happens? It is much better to openly admit your mistakes than to ignore them or cover them up. A cover-up (perceived or real) is probably the greatest single enemy to trust.

Tip Number 4. Establish strong business ethics. Business ethics is about setting moral values for the workplace. Ethical conduct is when there is alignment between the human behavior and this set of moral standards. In virtual teams, it is especially important that ethical standards are understood and internalized by each team member. These can be an important part of a team's operating guidelines (see Chapter 6, "Distance Team Building: Practical Tips for Building Effective Teams").

Teams with common ethics will be healthier, more productive, adaptable, responsive, and resourceful because they will be united under one common value set.

Tip Number 5. Do what you say you will do, and make your actions visible. Visibly keeping commitments increases trust. It doesn't take long for team members to pick up on insincere rhetoric or broken promises. Sometimes leaders neglect to make their actions visible to team members, thus creating the perception that they don't follow through. Instead of assuming that team members know you did something, tell them by saying "In response to your suggestions about such and such, I did such and such yesterday. Thanks for the recommendation." While this can happen in any team, distance magnifies the impact of a leader's perceived lack of action.

Tip Number 6. Make sure that your interactions with the team are consistent and predictable. The process of building trust is not an event—it is a process. Trust results from consistent and predictable interaction over time. If team members see a leader respond one way this week and another way next week, it becomes harder and harder to trust him or her.

Tip Number 7. From the outset, set the tone for future interaction. The initial actions of the leader set the tone and establish norms that can either build trust or detract from establishing trust within the team. For instance, Professor Sirkka L. Jarvenpaa of the University of Texas at Austin and Associate Professor Dorothy E. Leidner of INSEAD in Fontainebleau, France, discovered that in one case they studied, initial electronic communication had a profound impact on a virtual team's interaction throughout the life of the project: "... the appointed leader sent an introductory message with a distrustful tone, implying that he was suspicious of other members' commitment to the team. Throughout the project, the team was plagued by low morale and poor performance. Its members were never able to forge a trusting relationship."[2] We have long known that leading by example is almost always more powerful than speeches and lectures. This is a core behavior for the living example competency we introduced in Chapter 1. Virtual leadership is no different.

Tip Number 8. Be accessible and responsive. As mentioned in Chapter 3, find ways to make yourself regularly available to team members. This can be tricky when working across multiple time zones. Establishing a rotating schedule of in-person visits for different sites can help. Likewise, setting regular virtual meeting times (via teleconference, videoconference, etc.) provides team members with the assurance that there will be an opportunity to address questions or problems without a significant waiting period.

Even in a natural work group team or a co-located project team, where team members have opportunities for interaction (whether planned or unplanned) with the leader, unresponsiveness can cause uneasiness and eventually distrust, which is amplified by the distance factor. Be action oriented. Instead of saying, "let's think about it," say, "let's do this and that." And then do it. We worked with one distance manager who would pick up the phone and take action on your discussion while you were discussing it. As a result, he was perceived by others as being action-oriented and trustworthy.

When remote employees contact you by e-mail or voice mail, respond within 24 hours, unless it is obviously an emergency—and in that case respond immediately. If the team members are having their feet held to the fire to meet established timelines, they will look to the leader to quickly get them answers, information, or the OK to move ahead with a decision. Lack of timely response can look like sabotage to someone sitting thousands of miles away with a customer looking them in the eye, demanding an answer. Establish agreements up front with the team on how you will respond to them and in what time frame. Then honor those agreements throughout the life of the project or relationship.

Tip Number 9. Maintain confidences. Team members need to be able to express concerns, identify problems, share sensitive information, and surface relevant issues. Getting agreements early on as to how confidential or sensitive data will be handled is important. This can usually be effectively done as part of the operating guidelines discussion described in Chapter 6, "Distance Team Building: Practical Tips for Building Effective Teams."

Tip Number 10. Watch your language. In subtle ways a leader can unintentionally erode trust among his/her team members. Working from the home office and referring to team members in satellite offices as "them" or "those people" may send an unintended message. Jacklyn Kostner, in an interview in *Getting Results,* calls these "location-centric words and actions."[3] As she points out, this can get carried to an extreme when it moves from words to action and you start assigning all the exciting parts of the project to those close to home.

There are other issues around language, as well. Be sensitive to using home office or cultural slang that might not be understood by all team members. When terminology is used that someone doesn't understand, their sense of isolation is increased. For instance, when you hear words used in teleconferences, that may be unfamiliar to some, check for understanding and ask the speaker to clarify the meaning for others. Or when e-mails contain jargon or acronyms unique to a function, location, or culture, follow up with clarification and then coach team members to avoid using such terms in future communication.

Finally, it has become increasingly common in western business to use four-letter words that Mom might not approve of. Hearing a leader use what may be perceived as vulgarity or profanity or reading it in writing can be offensive to some. It's best to stick with common professional business language, especially when working across organizational or ethnic cultures.

Tip Number 11. Create social time for the team. In co-located teams, much of the trust and confidence that team members have in one another and in the leader comes from informal social interaction. For virtual teams to have this experience requires a little more thought and creativity. Perhaps the easiest way is to build informal socializing time into video or teleconferences. At either the beginning or the end of a call or meeting, lead the way with informal conversation, asking about team members' outside interests, families, etc.

Summary

Building trust in a virtual team involves meeting several challenges. With some thought and planning, however, these challenges can be overcome. Leading by example is undoubtedly the most powerful tool the distance manager has for building trust. Open and frequent communication builds the foundation. Giving trust to others paves the way for generating trust between team members and between the leader and the team. Likewise, being honest and doing what you say you'll do helps model the way for others. Additional trust-building include activities establishing strong business ethics within the team, ensuring that one's interactions with the team are consistent and predictable, thoughtfully setting the initial tone for interaction within the team, being responsive to team member requests or inquiries, monitoring language and terminology, maintaining confidences, and creating opportunities for social interaction among virtual team members. All of these tips sound deceptively simple, but each is remarkably effective in establishing a climate of trust and openness.

References

1. Diane L. Coutu, "Trust in Virtual Teams," *Harvard Business Review*, May–June 1998 v76 n3 p. 20.
2. Ibid.
3. Jacklyn Kostner, "Learn to be a Distance Manager," *Getting Results*, July 1997, v 42 n7, p. 6.

CHAPTER

Overcoming the Isolation of the Satellite Office

While some people will be comfortable working at home without any face-to-face contact with others, most human beings are social animals who need some type of interaction to maintain their morale and motivation. Whether this is obtained during coffee breaks, smoking breaks, or lunch, or at the water cooler, is unimportant: however, it is one part of the work environment that is eliminated in the virtual office.[1]

Thomas Greenbaum, President
Groups Plus, Inc.

AFTER AN IMPRESSIVE 20-year career that included stints at three *Fortune* 500 companies, Catherine (not her real name) was recruited to work for a small consulting firm as a satellite employee working from a remote site. At first the idea seemed exciting. The thought of more freedom, of being able to choose work hours, and of having the flexibility to schedule clients as she pleased were all part of the attraction. After a few months of "settling in" time, however, Catherine began feeling concerned. She felt a growing sense of isolation and yearned for the collegial atmosphere and close working relationships with respected colleagues she had left behind in her last company. As time moved on, the loneliness intensified. She missed having coworkers nearby who she could bounce ideas off of. She also felt "out of the loop" and often wondered what exactly was going on with the business. What new clients had come on board? What were other consultants learning and experiencing? It was funny, but she even found herself missing some of the more mundane and irritating parts of corporate life, such as budget reviews and planning meetings. She just plain missed being where "the action was"—having access to company happenings. And finally she really missed the informal contact and socializing that had been a normal part of an average workday. Within nine months, Catherine wondered if she had made a big mistake.

Catherine made an appointment with a research group in a nearby city that conducted tests and interviews to determine people's aptitude for certain kinds of work. The process concluded with an analysis intended to help the individual determine what disciplines might provide the most satisfying careers. After two days of testing and analysis, the research consultant sat down with Catherine to give her the results and recommendations. "What kind of work are you currently doing?" he asked first. Catherine explained her current setup and the kind of consulting work she was engaged in. When she was finished, the consultant looked pensive for a moment, then said: "You may want to reconsider that path. Based on our analyses, you are a very social individual who thrives on working closely with others. I would venture to say that *who* you work with is as important to your satisfaction as the work itself. In spite of your being an extremely delightful person, you just aren't enough for yourself. You really need to have considerable interaction with others."

Catherine isn't unique. Many people thrive on social interaction, and regardless of the touted benefits of working virtually, it will not be ideal for everyone. But in today's environment, more and more employees are being asked to work on dispersed teams or in isolated satellite offices with little day-to-day interaction with others.

Distance managers, therefore, are often called upon to help employees deal with these feelings of isolation. Team members who feel connected to the rest of the organization are much more likely to be productive and satisfied employees than those left with only e-mail and voice mail to keep them company. In this chapter we'll discuss some tips for helping isolated employees stay connected.

Selecting People for Satellite Operations

Carefully select those who will work alone for long periods. There are a few characteristics to look for when determining who should staff satellite locations or serve on geographically dispersed teams for an extended time. Those who tend to do best are those who like working alone but who aren't antisocial loners. Being placed in a remote office could be very detrimental to the self-professed "loner." The isolation could exacerbate the problems resulting from what may already be a self-imposed lack of contact with others, thus rendering him or her ineffective in making decisions, solving problems, or seizing opportunities for personal growth.

Second, and perhaps most obvious, individuals working in virtual settings need to be self-starters who require little prodding to keep projects or other work moving forward. Remember the wisdom of Doug Loewe, European marketing manager for CompuServe (see Chapter 1, "The Seven Competencies of an Effective Distance Manager"). Loewe, himself based in New York, manages a staff of 15 sales and support people in offices in Europe. Says he: "For someone who manages long-distance, it is crucial that his team is comprised of self-starters, people who have strong discipline. The salespeople must understand that working from home doesn't mean a break in the action or a chance to fool around. The system will fail if the team is made up of the type of people who need constant prodding to get the work done."[2]

Other characteristics or skills that independent workers should possess include:

1. *Technological competence.* In addition to basic technical skills, working virtually requires proficiency with communication tools such

as computers, e-mail, intranets, and so forth. If people in remote locations don't already have these basic skills, it will be difficult to train them in your specific applications.

2. *Good judgment.* Working across distance and time almost guarantees that individuals will be required to make critical decisions on their own. Thus, an ability to employ good judgment in a timely way is crucial.

3. *Good interpersonal skills.* This may sound surprising, but as we have noted in other chapters, an inability to work well with others can actually become magnified across distance. If an individual lacks the skills to interact successfully with others face-to-face, working with him or her remotely becomes a dreaded experience for everyone involved. This person may also become increasingly isolated and ineffective as others discover how easy it is to "lock" someone out when they aren't physically present.

4. *Willingness to take accountability for results—both personal and business.* Working in a satellite office or on a dispersed team isn't easy. Success depends in large measure on the individual's willingness to find ways to make it work. Initiating ways to share learnings with remote colleagues, rather than lamenting the fact that they aren't in the next cubicle, might be one example of this willingness to assume accountability. Individuals eager to make a less than ideal situation work are much more likely to succeed in a virtual setting than those prone to feeling like "victims" when things don't go their way.

Personality profiling tools are available that can provide insight into one's aptitude for working alone. These can be useful when used in conjunction with other tools such as adequate training. Be frank with people about the isolation that is common in these types of teams. Ask for examples of where they have successfully operated that way before, and listen to the way they talk about it. Do they sound happy? Sad? Frustrated? A rule of thumb in the behavioral sciences field is that past behavior is the best predictor of future behavior. If they loved working remotely before, they'll probably like it again. If they hated it, there may not be a lot you can do to help.

Tips for Helping Team Members Overcome Isolation

Once you have the right people in place, use the following tips to help team members overcome the isolation that is common in virtual teams:

Tip Number 1. Provide training for those going into remote working situations. Preparation is one of the keys to a successful transition to working in satellite locations. To assume that employees know what to expect and how to make the distance situation work is naive at best and more likely a recipe for failure.

Make certain the training provides a realistic picture of what it will be like working alone. Have people who have worked in similar situations provide their perspectives, both positive and negative. A panel discussion of individuals who have "virtual experience," with time allotted for questions and answers, can be very effective. You might want to also include a visit to a satellite office to provide a firsthand glimpse of the kind of setup and accompanying technology that makes a virtual situation workable.

Tip Number 2. Create "cyber cafes"[3] on your company intranet so virtual employees stay in touch and talk informally. As Catherine's experience illustrates, many satellite employees miss human contact or social connection the most. A sanctioned intranet chat room provides a vehicle for day-to-day interaction with colleagues that reduces the sense of isolation and can also foster creativity and learning across distance. This clearly helped the people in the ARC case described in Chapter 2.

Creativity and innovation are both greatly facilitated by social interaction and collaboration. Some organizations, such as Sun Microsystems in Menlo Park, California, have made a concerted effort, via architectural design, to encourage conversation and interaction among employees who are co-located. Sun's Menlo Park complex was designed with only 35 percent of the interior space dedicated to office space, and with 225 meeting places where engineers and others can meet to share ideas, stories, experiences, and so forth.[4]

An intranet chat room can serve a similar purpose for virtual teams. It provides a place for coworkers to meet and exchange ideas, get feedback, share learning experiences, and get a fresh perspective from others. It can protect both individuals and the corporation from losing their creative edge while still utilizing the benefits of smaller, satellite offices.

Tip Number 3. Encourage virtual team members to create "highway cafes." In a co-located world, the company cafeteria provides a natural and convenient place for corporate schmoozing, networking, or socializing to occur. Creating this same kind of opportunity for remote employees takes some effort but the payoff is worth it. One way for virtual team members to connect with others is via *highway cafes,* the corporate cafeterias of the virtual world. People like Renee Romeiser, a freelance Web and multimedia developer based in Warrenville, Illinois, find it important to maintain contacts by making time, like lunchtime, to network.[5] Similarly, sales reps working from different satellite locations might agree to meet at a designated restaurant to have lunch, share recent accomplishments or learnings, and do some needed professional socializing. Or a consultant working alone much of the time might schedule regular lunches with friends or former coworkers from different companies as a way of maintaining a reasonable level of human interaction and contact.

Tip Number 4. Avoid asking new employees to work virtually. Acquiring and assimilating information about one's organization is an important part of a new-hire's on-boarding process. This is much more difficult to do from remote sites. Further, not being given an initial opportunity to establish relationships with at least a few other employees puts the new-hire at a disadvantage. A new employee's ability to network is impaired when he or she doesn't know whom to contact or doesn't feel comfortable contacting someone he or she has never met.

In some cases, such as geographically dispersed sales teams, this may be unavoidable. In these cases, build in some face-to-face time for the employee up front—both with you as the distance manager and with his or her coworkers to allow the employee to establish relationships and get a feel for the culture.

Tip Number 5. Use a "hoteling" approach to office space. Rather than leave employees entirely on their own, working out of cars or home offices, some companies use what is called *hoteling.* In this scenario, employees can call ahead and reserve an office space for the day or for a few hours. This allows at least occasional office interaction.

IBM is one organization that uses these temporary offices, but in some cases they have tried to make them more personalized than most hoteling configurations. For example, at an IBM facility in Whitehouse Station, New Jersey, office spaces are provided on a first-come, first-served basis, with no guarantee that an individual will get the same one again. But as a way to foster a sense of personal space and office cohesion, a long wall is provided on which employees can display pictures and other personal items that one might find in a traditional office. All of this serves to provide a sense of belonging and to alleviate feelings of isolation.

"Teaming space," where coworkers share space on a mutually agreed-upon schedule, or "free space," in which individuals grab whatever work space is available, are other options for providing temporary office space for those working virtually.[6] Some organizations go even further. One Hewlett-Packard new-product development team put desks in the team office for satellite team members. Even though these desks would seldom be used by the distance team members, who often worked alone somewhere across the globe, this arrangement made both the isolated individual and the team members who were co-located feel like they all belonged to the same team.

Tip Number 6. Encourage virtual team members to use visual reminders of their virtual coworkers. Maybe a picture of the team, taken at that initial face-to-face meeting (see Chapter 12, "The Necessity of Face to Face Meetings") could be given to each member so they can keep it near their computer or telephone as a visual reminder of their teammates. Or a memento of a team-building session or special team meeting (e.g., a mug, plaque, etc.) can also serve to create a physical sense of "team."

Tip Number 7. Create a team Web page. In addition to a chat room or cyber cafe for informal communication with team members, or an extranet for virtual customer interaction, set up a Web page for virtual team members. Beyond providing a place for formal business communication and a repository for important records, it can provide a sort of shared identity for team members who don't interact frequently face-to-face. Consider putting team member photographs on the page. Some virtual teams even create team symbols or graphics which, like a corporate logo, provide an additional sense of identity.

Summary

Working virtually will result in at least occasional or mild feelings of isolation or loneliness for the majority of people. But there are steps the distance manager can take to minimize the impact of these feelings, starting with the careful selection of individuals who will operate this way. This includes avoiding the placement of newly hired employees immediately in a virtual situation. If possible, give them time to assimilate into the company culture and to establish relationships with you and their coworkers. Once the individuals are identified, providing good training and preparation for what lies ahead is imperative.

The day-to-day management of working virtually can be improved by a variety of techniques including creating cyber cafes and highway cafes as places for employees to gather and share ideas. Finally, using creative office setups such as hoteling, free space, and teaming space, along with establishing a sense of cohesion via visual artifacts, can all play a role in minimizing isolation and maximizing productivity.

References

1. Thomas L Greenbaum, "Avoiding a 'Virtual' Disaster," *HR Focus,* February 1998, p. 11. Reprinted by permission. © 1998. IOMA's HR Focus Report. (212) 244-0360 http://www.ioma.com/.
2. Doug Loewe, "Long-Distance Manager," *Sales & Marketing Management,* October 1994, p. 25.
3. Barbara B. Buchholz, "The Space Age," *Crain's Chicago Business,* June 7, 1999, p. E70.
4. Michael A. Verespej, "The Idea is to Talk," *Industry Week,* April 15, 1996, p. 28.
5. As quoted in "On Becoming Virtual," by Sacha Cohen, *Training & Development,* May 1997, p. 31.
6. Barbara B. Buchholz, "The Space Age," *Crain's Chicago Business,* June 7, 1999, p. E70.

CHAPTER

Managing Employees Who Work at Home

Working from home takes a certain kind of person. It isn't for everyone. If the social interactions and professional attire are important to you, this may not be for you.

Jill Freeman, Webmaster/Project Specialist
Weyerhaeuser Company

AFTER THE BIRTH of her second child, Jill Freeman, a Web-master/project specialist at Weyerhaeuser Company in Federal Way, Washington, decided to explore the possibility of working from home to accommodate lifestyle changes she and her family felt would better suit their situation. Almost five years later, Freeman speaks enthusiastically about the challenges and benefits of a work-at-home situation.

Many of the tips we have already reviewed can help the work-at-home team member stay connected and effective. But the distance workers and managers we work with have suggested a few additional tips that specifically aid those who maintain offices at home for a significant part of their work time. In this chapter we will review some recommendations for helping team members be more effective working out of home-based offices.

Do Home Offices Make Sense for Your Operation?

Decide if home offices will work for your operation. Before team members set up home offices, learn if this approach really makes sense for your business situation. Can the work be done remotely? How much on-site interaction with others is necessary to complete the tasks? Is the technology necessary to equip the home office worker cost-justified? Who will pay for it, maintain it, and own it?

Even if it makes sense to have people with remote home offices, remember that this workstyle isn't a good fit for everyone. Some people who think they would enjoy working from home find that they don't like it and aren't as productive as they thought they would be. Many find that their home situation isn't conducive to their particular work or that their personal need for interaction with others requires being around other team members on a regular basis.

Encourage team members to learn everything they can about work-at-home arrangements and their applicability to their personal situations. The success or failure of a work-at-home arrangement depends on personality, company support, family, peers, and customers, the availability of necessary technology, and the physical setup of the home office.

Jill Freeman spent months researching and reading everything she could find on working at home. She explains, "I thought about it, learned about it, and got up to speed on all aspects of working at home. This allowed me to make an efficient proposal to my work team." Having researched the topic thoroughly, Freeman was able to respond to the many questions the team asked when she first brought her proposal forward. The team also felt better prepared to move ahead and to support her in trying this different kind of working arrangement.

Encourage potential work-at-home team members to talk to others who are currently working from home or who have done so in the past. How do they deal with the isolation? Do they miss the social interaction of the on-site office? What processes have they put in place to stay "in the loop" with on-site employees? How does it feel not to don professional attire and be "at the office?" What issues have they encountered with their coworkers, manager, or customers? How has their family life been impacted? What technology has been most critical?

Tips for Helping Team Members Who Work at Home

Once the business and the individual agree that a home office operation makes sense, there are a number of things that you as distance manager can do to help this work situation be as productive as possible. Let's review some tips that will help the home worker integrate more effectively with other team members and be as effective as possible when working out of his or her home office.

Tip Number 1. Review the home office work arrangement regularly and formally with the on-site team members. This allows the team to address any problems or concerns that may arise due to having one or more team members off-site. In Freeman's case, the work-at-home arrangement was a regular agenda topic at many team meetings for the first year and a half that she was working from home. Both Freeman's concerns ("How can I stay in the loop?") and the team's concerns ("How can we contact Freeman when we need her?") were addressed and resolved.

Tip Number 2. Encourage home office workers to define their core work hours. While working from home allows some departure from traditional work routines, it nevertheless requires a minimum of structure, especially around work hours. Coworkers, customers, managers, and families all need clarity about availability. For example, Freeman's typical workday begins at about 6:45 A.M. That is when she turns on the computer and starts to work. However, since one of Freeman's stated objectives for this work arrangement was better home and family management, she has defined her core work hours as 9:30 A.M. to 5:30 P.M. This is when her coworkers and customers know they can reach her and when teleconferences or Web meetings are scheduled. Defining her hours this way allows her to take her oldest son to the bus stop and drop the youngest off at his preschool before settling into the workday. It also helps her children understand when Mommy is working and when she is not.

Clearly defining work hours goes hand in hand with determining which days or hours the home office worker will be on-site. Few work-at-home employees never go into the office. Most are on-site at least a few days a month, usually from one-half to one day per week. Again, clearly defining this allows affected peers and customers to plan face-to-face meetings or other interactions that require the team member to be on-site.

Tip Number 3. Home workers should have an office with a door. They need dedicated, efficient office space to define the territory between personal and work space. Working from home doesn't mean laying work out on the kitchen table each morning and hoping you don't pick up any of the leftover peanut butter or macaroni and cheese from last night's meal. A professional work area is as critical, if not more so, when working from home than when working on-site in a downtown office. As one work-at-home employee explained: "Being able to go into my office and close the door is critical to my productivity. It helps my family understand very clearly when I am working and can't be disturbed."

Tip Number 4. Have the right technology. Working from home is just like any other virtual work situation—it can only be successful if the right technology is in place. Getting the right technological setup may mean added cost for the work-at-home employee. Some companies will fund the costs associated with the setup (e.g., a second phone line, a broadband connection, a laptop computer, e-mail, Internet access), but others will not. Having the employee absorb the costs eliminates having to address tricky issues such as who owns the equipment/services, but it can be quite expensive. As a distance manager, make sure that these issues are negotiated and agreed upon up front to avoid confusion or conflict later.

Minimal technology support for working at home includes:

- Dedicated computer and business phone lines (or cable or DSL connections lines that won't restrict the work-at-home team member's ability to be on the Internet or receive a fax on the computer at the same time that he or she is talking to a client on the telephone)
- E-mail
- Voice mail
- Internet access
- Company intranet access

- High-quality printer
- Fax machine
- Ergonomically designed chair
- Desk or other dedicated working space

Depending on the job or specific circumstances, other helpful technology may include:

- Laptop computer
- Personal digital assistant
- Cell phone
- Company telephone card (this eliminates the need for expense statements and other reimbursement headaches)
- Small but high-quality copier

In addition to making sure that home office employees have adequate technology, some companies such as Merrill Lynch and Arthur Andersen inspect home offices for compliance with safety standards.[1]

Tip Number 5. Remember that a work-at-home arrangement is still a fairly significant change for most organizations and most employees. As Freeman explains, "People's attitudes can get in the way. The thing that concerns me most is when people imply that I'm not really working on the days I'm at home. And some people still aren't open to even trying to work with me in this [work-at-home] arrangement. This creates roadblocks that really don't need to be there. Some don't respect my days at home and will schedule meetings on those days, knowing that I either won't be able to attend or will need to rearrange my calendar. But I have to remember that this is a major cultural change, and flexibility goes two ways. I have to be flexible and willing to make occasional changes, too." The distance manager needs to be alert to these inevitable conflicts, coach the parties involved, and make sure that the issues are appropriately resolved.

Summary

Although work-at-home arrangements aren't for everyone, many teams have people who work from their home offices at least part of the time. A few tips will help this work arrangement be more productive. Specifically: (1) do your homework to ensure that this arrangement fits the needs of both the person and the organization; (2) review the work arrangement regularly with other team members; (3) clearly define core work days and hours; (4) have offices with doors; (5) have the right technology; and (6) remember that this is still a big change for everyone.

Reference

1. Anne Tergesen, "Making Stay-at-Homes Feel Welcome," *Business Week,* October 12, 1998, n3599 p. 155.

CHAPTER

Leading People Who Don't Report to You

After the game, the king and pawn go into the same box.[1]

Italian proverb

WHEN BOEING PUT together the product development team for the 777 aircraft, the company decided to include representatives from United Airlines, the FAA, engineering, manufacturing, and maintenance. Project leaders, therefore, had team members who did not report to them, or, in some cases, to anyone in Boeing. When an electric car was designed by a joint venture created from Hughes and Delphi engineers, project leaders often managed technical people from two different companies at the same time. Hewlett-Packard frequently uses people from Intel or other key vendors in problem solving or product development activities. Apple Computer used large numbers of contract employees from temporary agencies to manufacture their early portable models. Just about everybody today works with outside consultants, customers, or vendors on key projects. In the high-tech industry it isn't even unusual to have competitors working together on the same project. These situations pose a tremendous challenge for the distance leader who is used to leading people who report directly to him or her.

How do you manage a virtual team when you don't have the power of position and hierarchy? In this chapter we'll discuss this increasingly common dilemma of the distance leader.

Substitutes for Hierarchy

Without hierarchy as a power source, those who are asked to lead people who don't report to them must find other ways to get a task or project done. The good news is that you can. The power of position or title is one way to do things—but it's not necessarily the best way.

Edward Lawler, a respected and prolific author of management theory, talks about "substitutes for hierarchy"—that is, infrastructures that can be used by leaders in place of hierarchy to direct and coordinate the workforce. It is interesting to note that leaders who are skilled at accomplishing things without relying on position power tend to be more effective regardless of whether they have position power. Consequently, the following substitutes for hierarchy—while crucial for those leading people who don't report to them—can help leaders in *any* situation to be more effective.

Tips for Leading People Who Don't Report to You

Tip Number 1. Use persuasion and influence instead of commands. Although you can simply issue orders when people report to you, you can't use this technique when they don't. In fact, ordering people around isn't very effective even when you have position power. Telling others what to do implies that they are subordinate to you. The hard sell ("I'll keep talking until you see it my way") erodes persuasiveness and can be viewed as manipulative. Other approaches that erode one's ability to be persuasive include: (1) resisting compromise ("my way or the highway"), which can erode relationships and suggests inflexibility or lack of creativity; (2) being unkind, negative, or impatient; and (3) being overly emotional (although appropriate emotional and empathic connection is useful).

Jay Conger, in his book on persuasion entitled *Winning 'Em Over,* states that in order to persuade others, one must first establish *credibility.* As

Conger points out, credibility is a function not only of expertise but also of the relationship one establishes with the person or persons he or she is trying to persuade.[2] Technical competence alone will not establish credibility if you don't have the skills necessary to create a good relationship. The world is full of people who are technically competent but who get passed over for key assignments because they aren't skilled in developing relationships. Being polite, employing good listening skills, and showing that you genuinely respect the other person(s) and their work will go a long way in establishing the credibility that facilitates persuasion—whether or not the person you are trying to persuade reports to you.

Tip Number 2. Use facts and data. The most effective kind of power is *information power* rather than position power. Having facts and data on your side is much more compelling than hierarchical clout. It is, for example, far more motivating to say, "I think we need to do this because our customers require it, the government mandates it, and competitors are doing it," than to say (or imply), "Do this because I'm the boss." Numerical data, historical evidence, research, and real examples are all more convincing than orders based on title or position.

Tip Number 3. Respect the expertise of all team members. A common phenomenon when crossing department or organization lines is an increased sense of loyalty to one's own roots. This has some positive benefits and may even be necessary to ensure that different issues are fairly represented. When manifested by the leader, however, it can have the unfortunate consequence of failing to acknowledge and fully utilize the expertise of all members. Find ways to involve other people as a way to tap into their expertise and experience. Asking for their participation is the highest form of respect.

Tip Number 4. Establish common ground. Before Yitzhak Rabin and Yasir Arafat signed the Israeli-Palestinian Declaration of Principles in September 1993, many people believed the conflict to be irresolvable. Facilitators like Brigham Young University professor Bonner Ritchie who were involved in the peace process met with the opposing parties to see if there wasn't something on which they could agree. Although the two leaders had nearly intractable differences on issues associated with dividing land ownership, government responsibilities, and other issues associated with reducing violence in the area, there was one thing that they discovered to be common ground: Both loved their children and wanted someday to provide a place where those children could enjoy peace.

While the issues involving these factions are still far from resolved, the motivating factor that has allowed them to continue to work towards resolution is their common love for children.

Organizations with far less conflict than this also find this approach to be useful. When management and unions, for example, have strong disagreement on matters of policy, they still have common ground in preserving the safety of the work force. Similarly, groups with membership from different companies may differ significantly in their basic organizational philosophies, reward and recognition systems, and approaches to problem solving, but they still can find common ground around things such as satisfying customer requirements or meeting certain financial targets.

In his classic work, *Discovering Common Ground*, Marvin Weisbord describes how, through the use of strategic conferences in which achieving common ground plays a key role, groups of individuals from diverse backgrounds come together to do joint planning and problem solving. Weisbord explains the approach to such conferences:

> **When we invite the right people, we will nearly always find unresolved conflicts and disagreements. Yet we discourage conferees from "working" their differences. . . . Indeed, we neither avoid nor confront the extremes. Rather, we put our energy into staking out the widest common ground all can stand on without forcing or compromising. Then, from that solid base, we spontaneously invent new forms of action, using processes devised for that purpose.**
>
> **In short, we seek to hear and appreciate differences, not reconcile them. We seek to validate polarities, not reduce the distance between them. We learn, innovate and act from a mutual base of discovered ideas, world views, and future goals. Above all, we stick to business. We make the conferences' central task our guiding star.[3]**

Given the differences that distance teams may include, this isn't a bad model. Acknowledge differences, work to find the widest common ground, then stick to the task at hand.

Tip Number 5. Maintain confidentiality. In Chapter 8 we discussed the importance of maintaining confidences as one of the keys to building trust in virtual teams. When leading individuals who don't report to you and who may represent different organizations, this becomes even more critical. Knowing that proprietary information, all confidential data, and personal concerns or issues will be handled respectfully, helps forge stronger, more productive relationships.

Within different corporate cultures—even different groups within the same company—ways of dealing with confidential information may vary dramatically. It's a good idea to discuss up front what constitutes confidential information and develop protocols for handling such data. An ideal time to have this conversation is during the operating guidelines discussion (see Chapter 8, "Building Trust from a Distance").

Tip Number 6. Exercise conscientiousness and integrity. If a leader can't use position power, he or she can still influence through moral authority. Research[4] indicates that leaders who demonstrate the characteristics of both conscientiousness and integrity (see Figure 11.1) are far more likely to get good results than those who do not display these characteristics. Our experience, buttressed by stories from other distance managers, strongly suggests that this is true whether the leader has position authority over those he or she directs or not.

Conscientiousness	Integrity
1. High achievement orientation	1. Honest actions, words, and emotions
2. Self-starting	
3. Takes initiative	2. Consistent behavior
4. Has focused objectives	3. Doesn't compromise values
5. Proactive	4. Clearly articulates values
6. Believes that he or she can make a difference	5. Actions aligned with values
	6. Honest with self
7. Deals with problems	7. Nonmanipulative
8. Doesn't make excuses	8. Dependable
9. Results-oriented	9. Trustworthy
10. Improvement bias	10. Has honor in the workplace
11. Doesn't blame others	11. Has honor out of the workplace

Figure 11.1   Examples of Conscientiousness and Integrity
Adapted from the Team Resource training program, The Fisher Group, Inc. © 2000. All rights reserved. Used with permission.

Conscientious leaders are high achievers and self-starters who take initiative and have focused objectives. Those who are conscientious have a "want to" and "choose to" rather than "have to" or "ought to" attitude. When issues arise, they deal with them. The conscientious leader doesn't make excuses for problems or poor performance; rather he or she works to resolve or improve them. In terms of the competencies introduced in Chapter 1, the conscientious leader is a results catalyst.

Leaders with integrity are honest and consistent about what they say, do, and feel. They have a clear set of values that they will not compromise, and they are nonmanipulative, dependable, and trustworthy. The leader with integrity is one who has mastered the competency of being a living example.

Interestingly, *both* conscientiousness and integrity are required to correlate to positive results. A conscientious leader without integrity may be more focused on the good of his or her project or career than on important organizational values. Conversely, the nonconscientious leader with integrity may have tremendous values and vision but create very little progress toward accomplishing them.

Summary

Leading people who don't report to you calls for an approach different from the traditional reliance on hierarchical or position power to get things done. Using "substitutes for hierarchy" allows the leader to accomplish tasks and complete projects in a manner that demonstrates respect for all factions. Conscientiousness and integrity and a willingness to maintain confidentiality, coupled with the use of persuasion, information and data, and common ground are among the substitutes for hierarchy that allow the distance manager who is leading individuals not "under his or her command" to be successful.

References

1. Novasoft Quotationary™ CD, 1999.
2. Jay A. Conger, *Winning 'Em Over: A New Model for Management in the Age of Persuasion,* New York: Simon & Schuster, 1998.
3. Marvin R. Weisbord and 35 international coauthors, *Discovering Common Ground: How Future Search Conferences Bring People Together to*

Achieve Breakthrough Innovation, Empowerment, Shared vision, and Collaborative Action, San Francisco: Berrett-Koehler, 1992, p. 7. Reprinted with permission of the publisher. From *Discovering Common Ground* copyright © 1992 by Weisbord, Berrett-Koehler Publishers, Inc., San Francisco, California. All rights reserved. 1-800-929-2929.

4. Robert P. Tett, "Is Conscientiousness ALWAYS Positively Related to Job Performance?" for the Society of Industrial and Organizational Psychology, as posted on www.siop.org/tip/backissues/TIPJuly98/tett.htm.

The Necessity of Face-to-Face Meetings

Social interaction is really important—you can't eliminate it—you can't do everything virtually. The challenge is to interact rapidly and effectively.

Richard A. Thier, Manager, Organization Effectiveness
Xerox

XEROX HAS CREATED a nine-step model for developing effective virtual teams. It includes the following: (1) form the team, (2) communicate the vision, (3) develop a mission statement, (4) define goals, (5) develop norms, (6) develop roles, (7) develop meeting processes, (8) develop communication processes, and (9) develop work processes (see Figure 12.1). Xerox illustrates the model in a stairstep format with the first stair at the bottom and the last one at the top. According to internal virtual team guru Richard Thier, teams that go through this start-up process are *significantly* more likely to be successful than those that

9. Develop work processes

8. Develop communication processes

7. Develop meeting processes

6. Develop roles

5. Develop norms

4. Define goals

3. Develop a mission statement

2. Communicate the vision

1. Form the team

Figure 12.1   The Xerox Model for Developing Virtual Teams

take a less disciplined approach. But almost all of this start-up process requires face-to-face interaction.

Terms such as *virtual team* and *distance manager* imply that these are teams or individuals that never come together physically. In reality, however, a clear majority of those who work in virtual settings strongly advocate having some face-to-face time. While improvements in technology may one day render such a notion a waste of time and money, current work practices still deem it a good idea. A caution is in order at this point. Face-to-face meetings are not inherently superior to virtual ones (as we will illustrate in Chapter 25, "The Distance Product Development Manager at Hewlett-Packard.") There are some times when the purpose of a meeting is better and more efficiently met virtually. But most people in virtual teams tend to not have enough face-to-face interaction, rather than the other way around.

One author maintains that face-to-face meetings are appropriate "(1) when you need the richest nonverbal cues, including body, voice, proximity...; (2) when the issues are especially sensitive; (3) when the people don't know one another; (4) when establishing group rapport and relationships are crucial; and (5) when the participants can be in the same place at the same time." She points out that one of the great advantages of face-to-face meetings is that they are "less technologically complex and therefore their systems are easier to use, less likely to crash, and less likely to have compatibility problems."[1]

In this brief chapter on face-to-face meetings, we will focus on the most common times and circumstances where coming together provides considerable gain for the team. We will consider three important meetings: the kickoff, milepost, and wrap-up/celebration activities, as well as other events such as performance reviews and conflict-resolution sessions which normally require face-to-face interaction.

Kickoff Meeting

Effective teams almost universally attribute at least part of their success to getting off to a good start. A poor start-up is one of the five potential derailers for the distance leader mentioned in Chapter 2 ("Five Things That Will Cripple the Effectiveness of the Distance Manager"), and achieving a good start-up has been mentioned in Chapter 6 ("Distance Team Building: Practical Tips for Building Effective Teams") as a key intervention.

Sitting together face-to-face to define the team's charter, set goals, establish operating guidelines, describe communication preferences, and review boundaries helps a group to coalesce and begin establishing trust. The team-chartering exercise gives the members of the virtual team a clear and common understanding of their purpose. Why is this important? Because automatically achieving a common understanding of purpose is unusual when you first bring a team of people together. Team members tend to have their own ideas of what the team is supposed to do, and those ideas may be contradictory. In one organization where we worked, for example, some of the engineers on the team thought that their primary purpose was to create state-of-the-art products. Other engineers on the same team thought their primary purpose was to create products required by the customer. It wasn't until team members could sit down face-to-face and discuss the different options that they were able to come to an agreement that saved hours of productivity that might have otherwise been wasted.

Having this kind of conversation face-to-face is what makes it so valuable. Being face-to-face allows team members to have a more meaningful exchange and to engage each other early on in discussion and to debate factors critical to the team's success.

Milepost Meetings

Keeping virtual team members focused and coordinated can be difficult. But bringing together an entire team or representatives from each site on a regular basis (or at critical points in a project) can greatly improve such efforts. Distance managers we interviewed suggested midproject and end-of-project face-to-face meetings as a minimum. Midproject reviews, for instance, allow people to calibrate. They provide a forum for addressing current or potential problems and allow team members to stay emotionally connected as well as "task connected." If your team isn't driven by a project, some regularly established time period—say once every quarter—will do the same thing.

Wrap-Up or Celebration Meetings

Not only can wrap-up meetings serve to mark the end of a project or activity, they can also prepare the team to be more effective in future assignments. A face-to-face discussion of learnings from a project allows people to build on one another's ideas more effectively than a virtual meeting would. Deeper discussion can ensue, which offers all participants the opportunity to take an objective but critical look at decisions that were made, problems that were solved, issues that were addressed, and actions that were taken.

A face-to-face celebration of accomplishments provides well-earned recognition for the team and for individual team members. It also gives the team closure on the project and allows its members to mentally prepare for the next assignment.

In addition to these meetings, other situations may arise that require face-to-face time. These include:

Performance Reviews

Discussing a team member's overall performance and his or her contribution to the team and the organization warrants a face-to-face session. Hearing about one's performance via e-mail, voice mail, or even teleconference or videoconference can diminish the impact of the conversation. A leader willing to spend the time, effort, and money to have a face-to-face discussion sincerely and convincingly conveys his or her appreciation for the team member's effort as well as the manager's commitment to coach that person.

Other Performance Discussions

When addressing poor performance or behaviors requiring corrective action, face-to-face conversations are almost always more effective. Discussions that include significant emotional content should take place when people can establish eye contact and have the advantage of reading body language and other subtle nuances. Establishing rapport and communicating one's support are critical elements of these conversations that are difficult to accomplish without being face-to-face.

Conflict Resolution

When striving to resolve conflict within the team or between the team and other parties, it is much better to interact on a face-to-face basis. (See Chapter 9, "Distance Team Building: Practical Tips for Building Effective Teams" for some ideas on how to approach these sessions.) As with performance correction or improvement discussions, dealing successfully with conflict requires building rapport and having the opportunity to make eye contact and read body language.

Summary

There are a few key times when meeting face-to-face is strongly preferred to communicating electronically. These situations include kick-off sessions, meetings to discuss key milestones, and wrap-up or celebration get-togethers. Additionally, when giving performance feedback or attempting to resolve conflict, in-person sessions are considerably more effective.

Some will argue that now or in the near future technology will entirely replace the need for individuals to meet face-to-face. Almost everyone we interviewed, however, stated that while that may be technologically possible, it will not be preferable. The dynamics of a face-to-face conversation, they maintain, can never be fully transplanted by technology.

Reference

1. Mary Munter, "Meeting Technology: From Low-Tech to High-Tech," *Business Communication Quarterly*, June 1998, p. 80. Reprinted with the permission of the Association for Business Communication.

Celebrating from a Distance

The first responsibility of a leader is to define reality. The last is to say thank you. In between, the leader is a servant.[1]

Max DuPree, CEO
Herman Miller, Inc.

MOST WOULD AGREE that celebrating the success of a project or an individual's achievement is an important part of the manager's role. Celebrations are a way to validate learning, have fun, and say thank you. As with most other aspects of virtual managing, however, celebration across distance is more difficult than having an office party with co-located workers. In this chapter we will offer a dozen tips for distance celebrations.

Tips for Distance Celebrations

Tip Number 1. Celebrate both team and individual accomplishments. Contributions are made at both the group and the individual level, so it makes sense to recognize and celebrate both. In today's business world, where teams have taken hold as a primary organizational structure, it is sometimes wrongly assumed that celebrating and recognizing can only be done for the whole group and that there is something almost sacrilegious about focusing on the individual. But both approaches are appropriate, depending on the circumstance. Be sensitive, however, to recognizing an individual if the accomplishment included other people. That's where you can run into some problems.

Tip Number 2. Celebrate mileposts. Don't limit celebrations to the big finish. This is especially critical in virtual teams in order to keep motivation and morale high, since individuals can't give one another "high fives" on a daily basis. You don't have to have a big event to celebrate. Send everybody a thank-you e-card once in a while. Leave a voice mail message saying how much you appreciate something. Pop a $15 gift certificate in the mail after a good meeting or positive customer response. In *Fortune's* "The 100 Best Companies to Work for in America," the authors note that almost everything these companies do (even their normal daily correspondence) has a celebratory feel to it.[2]

Tip Number 3. Include face-to-face celebrations. As discussed in Chapter 12, "The Necessity of Face-to-Face Meetings," we strongly recommend that virtual coworkers come together at least once or twice during a project—at the beginning or when the team is first formed, and again when the team is disbanded or the task is completed. Both of these occasions can include celebration. The first session celebrates the inception of the group and/or the project or task they are about to undertake. The last meeting includes acknowledgment and celebration of the successful completion of the task or project or the fulfillment of the team's purpose. This last meeting is very important because it provides closure for all those involved and allows them to mentally prepare for their next assignment.

Tip Number 4. Hold an annual or semiannual goal achievement review activity. This gives the group an opportunity to examine their achievements and to refocus on their goals. Try to make this more than the usual routine presentation format, especially if you are doing it electronically or via videoconference. You might spoof the Academy Awards by distributing Oscars or other customized awards. We work with one client that keeps small presents in the back of the room during face-to-face meetings. These can be given by any team member to any other team member at any time of the meeting. For example, in a recent meeting one team member pulled a toy airplane out of the gift pile to give to another team member for expressing a thought that "flew high above" the others. Another gave some golden nugget candy to someone for "making a valuable contribution." It was fun and it made people laugh.

Tip Number 5. Respect personal preferences when deciding how to celebrate. What may constitute a reward or positive recognition for one may be the opposite for another. For example, a presentation to a senior manager may be seen by one team member as a rewarding way to get more exposure in the company, while to another it may be a punishing waste of time and energy. At one high-tech company an employee threatened to quit when she learned that the manager was planning to give her a special individual recognition award. "I couldn't have done it without the rest of the team," she said, and was adamant that others on the team be given equal credit for the outcome. To be singled out would have been an embarrassment for her. Do some investigative work to learn what team members enjoy or the kinds of celebration activities they might appreciate. One of the keys to effective celebration is that the process is seen as relevant and valuable to those involved.

If your team crosses cultural distances, remember that what is celebratory to one individual may be offensive to another. While some may appreciate the gift of a bottle of wine, for example, that may be inappropriate for a Muslim or Mormon team member.

Tip Number 6. Create a place on your intranet for posting best practices and learnings. This is what Xerox and other companies do on a regular basis. The opportunity to share your learnings or have your process or approach posted as a best practice is a subtle but effective way to celebrate accomplishments. Not only does the team or individual receive recognition, but team members are able to learn from one another as well.

Tip Number 7. Celebrate the "small" stuff. One way to help remote employees feel connected and a part of something bigger than their one-desk office is to acknowledge personal milestones such as birthdays, anniversaries, weddings, child births, a recent accomplishment such as completing schooling, or their contribution to a community effort. While such achievements may have very little, if anything, to do with work, they are a significant part of what makes each of us who we are. This kind of acknowledgement sends a message that each person is recognized as more than an e-mail or voice mail address. Celebrating these personal passages can be another way to build cohesion in a dispersed team. Knowing about each other's achievements, however small, helps build camaraderie and respect, even from afar.

Tip Number 8. Use "portable parties." If you know that a special milestone is coming up that you will celebrate via teleconference or videoconference, put together a "party kit" and send one to each team member. You might include party hats, horns, confetti, party favors, certificates of achievement, or small inexpensive gifts or mementos that somehow represent the project, task, or specific milestone. Ask everyone to bring their party kit to the meeting and then do a verbal (or physical, if on videoconference) check to make certain everyone has their party supplies. It may sound like a silly idea, but a little light-hearted fun can be helpful and even healthful if the group has been under a lot of pressure.

Tip Number 9. Use e-gift certificates. Much of what virtual teams do is accomplished electronically, so providing e-gift certificates can be somewhat symbolic. Take these along with you when you make visits to remote sites and hand them out spontaneously to acknowledge specific accomplishments you discover while on-site.

Tip Number 10. Include others in the celebration, whether electronically or face-to-face. For instance, when sending an e-mail acknowledgment of an individual's or team's recent accomplishment, copy senior managers, executives, or the on-site coworkers of each individual. If you are having a face-to-face celebration, invite senior leaders or coworkers from other departments or groups to drop by and deliver their congratulations. If not, have them make a video you can attach to a celebratory e-mail.

Tip Number 11. Invest personal time to make celebrations and recognition more meaningful. When a leader puts in personal time and energy to recognize or celebrate accomplishments, it makes the celebration much more meaningful. In an *Industry Week* article, Shari Caudron notes: "Managers should recognize the power of their physical presence. Employees like frequent contact with their managers, however brief, because it subtly indicates that the manager recognizes the importance of their work.[3]

For distance managers, opportunities for such person-to-person interface are rare. Caudron goes on to suggest that "if in-person recognition of employees is impossible for some reason, managers should write personal notes about their performance. This demonstrates that the manager not only recognized they did a good job, but that their work was so good that he or she felt it necessary to take the time to tell them so in writing. Additionally, because written congratulations are tangible, the 'feel-good' benefits last much longer."[4]

Tip Number 12. Ask the team members how they would like to celebrate. When all else fails, go to the source. Often overlooked is the fact that those involved probably have some great ideas about how they would like to celebrate a milestone or wrap up a major project. If you are stumped about how to pull off a celebratory activity, ask the group. First determine if there are any boundary conditions (e.g., no one can travel) and share those up front before the group starts brainstorming.

Summary

Celebration keeps people going. It shows that the effort by each individual is recognized and appreciated. Although celebrating across time, space, and culture can be challenging, it can also be fun. The tips discussed in this chapter can help teams achieve the "fun" part and minimize the challenges. Including some face-to-face celebration time is highly recommended. Also, celebrating mileposts, holding goal achievement review activities, and creating a place for recognition on the team's or company's intranet can all help in overcoming distance factors. Other ideas to enhance fun include acknowledging personal preferences when deciding how and what to celebrate, celebrating personal milestones as well as team and organizational accomplishments, and including people outside the team to add another dimension to the recognition. Go out on a limb and do something different, like portable parties or e-gift certificates. Also, don't hesitate to invest some time and energy to make the celebration personal. Finally, go to the source—ask the team members what and how they would like to celebrate.

References

1. Novasoft Quotationary™ CD, 1999.
2. Shelly Branch, et al., "The 100 Best Companies to Work for in America," *Fortune,* February 1, 1999, Vol. 139.
3. Shari Caudron, "The Top 20 Ways to Motivate Employees," *Industry Week,* April 3, 1995, v244 n 7 p. 12.
4. Ibid.

3

The Distance Technology Handbook

Setting Up a Virtual Office: The Basic Hardware and Communication Lines People Need

Getting the right technology is only 10 percent of the solution. You have to get people trained on the technology.

Mark Armentrout, Manager of Information Technology
Arco Exploration and Production

Mark Armentrout is an information technology executive for a company that has used distance management for years to coordinate scientists, construction specialists, and production workers in a variety of fields. As the champion for an intensive internal study on effective team technology, he has strong opinions on what helps distance workers accomplish five basic tasks. The tasks are: (1) create effective virtual teams, (2) get the data they need, (3) share their learnings with each other, (4) facilitate technology transfer, and (5) make cycle time reductions. In Armentrout's research on these five critical topics, he discovered that it was not the technologies selected as much as the way the technologies are used that leads to competitive advantage. In this chapter we will review some tips for both of these areas of concern. Specifically, let's consider basic technology choices for setting up a virtual office properly and then also review some recommendations on how to use the technologies to their fullest advantage.

For team members to work effectively from their homes or from a remote office, they must have the appropriate equipment. Although the specific type of hardware and communication lines they need will vary from business to business (depending on technologies available at your location, needs to integrate with existing technologies, your and your teams' personal preferences, customer requirements, corporate mandates, and a host of other things), there are some basic recommendations that are appropriate for the vast majority of virtual offices. Since technologies change so rapidly that specific recommendations on software and hardware would probably become obsolete before this book gets printed, we will endeavor to provide more general observations that will be useful to distance leaders. See Figure 14.1 for the basic set-up recommendation. As you can see in this figure, we have made recommendations for individual virtual office team members, road warriors (the people who rarely come into an office), site recommendations (each separate office location), and business recommendations (for a collection of sites that work together). Rather than repeat all of the material listed in this figure, let's review some important additional considerations for establishing a virtual office.

Tips for Getting the Right Technology for Your Virtual Team

Tip Number 1. The best solution isn't always the most expensive or current one. Let's begin with a general observation. The latest whiz-bang technology may not always be the one that is right for you. Fit is more important than features. Do you *really need* all of the options on that system? Anticipating future needs is one thing, but getting things you'll never use is another. Overbuying technology may cause lost productivity when team members are forced to learn another program or trou-

For each virtual office person:	For each road warrior:	For each site:	For each business:

• Personal computer with:
  E-mail
  Software
  Internet access
  Intranet access
• Telephone with voice mail
Optional:
• Camera for Web video-conferencing
	• Laptop with:
	  FAX
	  E-mail
	  Software
	  Internet access
	  Intranet access
	• Cell phone with voice mail
	Optional:
	• Portable printer
		• Network
		• Printer(s)
		• Server
		• FAX
		• Teleconference equipment
		• Internet connection
		Optional:
		• Broadband connection and firewall
		• Video-conferencing equipment
			• Intranet
			Optional:
			• Extranet

Figure 14.1   The Basic Equipment for a Virtual Office

bleshoot all of the potential conflicts it may have with your current system. What's the bottom line? Get what you really need, not necessarily what is in vogue, what consultants are selling, or what appears to be potentially promising. Sometimes the older technology, or a slight modification to your current system, is plenty good enough.

Tip Number 2. Consider how effectively technologies will fit into your system, not how they will work as a stand-alone component. Virtually all technologies, ranging from simple telephones to complex software applications, are part of a whole system that must interface as seamlessly as possible with the other parts of that system. As we have mentioned before, this includes both a human and a technical side. Software is a good example. Many distance leaders have warned us that just because a program works well by itself, that doesn't mean that it will work well in your system. It may conflict with other software you have or be too new to interface properly with your operating system. It may also require training employees in its proper use.

Finding out how technologies operate by themselves is of little value. What works in someone else's system might not work in yours at all. Get some good advice from experts on how the technologies you and your team are considering work within the context of both your social and technical systems. If companies gained nothing else from the Y2K fire drill, many of them learned that their technical systems are more complex and interrelated than they thought they were.

Tip Number 3. Provide a reliable telephone system with voice mail. Even in our advanced technological age, the core communication technology for most virtual teams is still the telephone. Ensure that there is a good telephone system in place, with a service that allows callers to leave a voice mail message for anyone working in the office. Voice mail is important for teams that cross time, space, and culture because it allows asynchronous messages that can carry more emotional content than a written e-mail.

Tip Number 4. Get enough telephone capacity. Remember that not all areas in the world have high-quality telephone line services available to them. But at a minimum try to get telephone service that is of sufficient quality and capacity to enable you to transmit either voice or data (for connecting to the Internet or intranet) on it.

Even small virtual offices generally have multiple lines so that all team members can be on the phone, be on the Internet, and/or receive a fax simultaneously. This allows them to do things like look up an order on your intranet while talking to a customer. If you get the broadband communication linkup mentioned in the next tip, however, you will not need as many separate lines. Small offices in particular may require only enough lines to enable each team member to talk on the phone at the same time. All data transmissions may be able to be handled on a single line.

Tip Number 5. Establish a broadband communication network. Many offices are finding that they can't meet their communication needs without some type of broadband solution. Broadband connections, unlike normal telephone connections, can handle a great deal of traffic with much higher speeds. They are very important for things like hosting Internet Web pages or allowing multiple users simultaneous and fast network interaction. A current favorite is DSL because it allows a dedicated line that is fairly cost effective, rather than other very expensive dedicated services like T1 lines, or solutions such as current cable connections, whose transmission speed is affected by the number of people using the line at the same time. As with most of the tips in this chapter, it's a really good idea to double-check with an information technology consultant to help you determine (1) how important a broadband solution is for your office, and (2) which solution best meets your needs.

Tip Number 6. Establish good-quality teleconference capability. The office should have a good-quality speaker phone capability so that team members can have real-time teleconferences with you, customers, and other virtual team members. Get the right teleconference equipment for you (i.e., phones with built-in speaker phones are adequate and more cost-effective in some situations, but separate teleconference equipment is better if you frequently do teleconferences with more than one person at a telephone). Establish teleconference capability (this can usually be done through your telephone system provider as either a regular or a periodic service option if your company doesn't have its own internal system). Train people how to set up teleconferences with multiple parties. It doesn't do much good to have the teleconference capability if people don't know how to use it.

Tip Number 7. Use communication equipment (e.g., cell phones, pagers, etc.) that severs the office tether. Team members who spend time away from the office will probably also need pagers and/or cell phones, and in certain remote locations without established cell networks they may even need satellite phones. For team members that spend regular time on the phone, a good-quality headset is also an excellent investment. This allows team members to walk around or use their hands to operate a computer while also reducing the head and neck strain common with many handheld telephones.

For team members who work from their cars, remember to provide hands-free cell phone systems. Holding a phone to your ear while you drive is dangerous.

Many distance workers eagerly await the day when a totally integrated personal communication device will be available to substitute for the pager/cell phone, personal computer, computer projector, palm-sized organizer, and other equipment they juggle on their way through the airport—but as of this writing it doesn't yet exist.

Tip Number 8. Determine what software you'll need before you determine what hardware to use. Your work should dictate your tools rather than your tools dictating your work. To facilitate this, look first at the tasks that need to be done and at the software necessary to do them. Consider typical projects. Do they involve database management? Report writing? Financial analysis? Developing presentations? How will team members use electronic support to communicate with you, customers, and each other? What corporate software programs are prescribed? Do you require specific software for your interfaces with other people (e.g., an ERP, company intranet, vendor extranet, organizational communication system)?

At a minimum you'll probably need basic business software including: (1) word processing, (2) spreadsheet analysis, (3) presentation development, (4) an e-mail program, and (5) Internet access. Many of these programs now come preloaded on the computers you would buy. But you may also need a calendar program, graphics/desktop publishing software, customer database management, CAD/CAM programs, video editing, and so forth.

Match the computer to the software requirements. If you do video, photography, or any graphics work like three-dimensional programming, you'll need a *lot* more memory than if you only do word processing. Consider not only what platform you should select, but review the operating system requirements, memory needs, and various interface options supported or required by your software. If an information technology resource is available to you, consult with them about your needs. And don't forget to include employees in these discussions. No one knows better than they do what support is necessary in order for them to do their jobs.

Tip Number 9. Standardize software versions. If you do nothing else with software, distance leaders advise that you standardize not only the software products that you buy, but that you also buy and maintain the same version of that product throughout the network. "If you use Microsoft Office," says Mark Armentrout, "you all need the same version." This minimizes compatibility problems and simplifies training and maintenance.

Tip Number 10. Buy every team member a personal computer. It is difficult to imagine any distance worker who doesn't need access to a computer. Current software enables team members to share space and files on a common computer if budget constraints demand, but the distance leaders we talked to advised against that. "For a personal computer to be an effective tool it has to be just that—personal," said one distance leader of a consulting team. "Having to coordinate access to a common computer affects productivity and makes it more difficult for people to get familiar and comfortable with their equipment." With the costs of computers becoming so reasonable, you would really have to be in a serious financial bind to be willing to put up with the problems associated with computer sharing. Don't do it unless your team members require only occasional access to one. If finances are a problem, you are generally better off to get an older machine for each team member than to spend the same money to buy a few new computers for people to share.

Think of both current and future needs when making your computer selections. Buying inexpensive computers that don't have enough memory or aren't upgradable could force you to replace your entire network in a matter of months as it becomes unable to run the latest software you'll need. Try to anticipate needs as much as possible and allow for some adaptability and growth.

Tip Number 11. Build a computer network. There is very little advantage to having each person's computer operate as a stand-alone machine. Build networks. Linking your computers together into a network saves costs (using shared peripherals like printers, data storage, etc.) and aids communication and collaboration. Although you don't have to have every one on the team use the same type of computer in order to create a network, most organizations prefer it that way. This reduces compatibility problems, streamlines maintenance work, and makes it easier to purchase software and plan systemwide upgrades.

A simple network may include a few Internet-ready computers linked together into a local area network (LAN) to share files with each other and to access shared Internet services and a common printer. A more elaborate system might have the computers linked via ethernet to a server (a separate computer available to everyone, where shared programs and files are kept), broadband Internet access (so everybody can be on the Web at the same time), multiple printer options (color or black-and-white, etc.), additional peripherals (scanner, hard disk backup, etc.), and remote machines (computers from off-site team members and the portable computers team members use when they are on the road). Some home offices build networks by using existing in-wall telephone lines to link two or three computers, and some virtual offices are experimenting with a variety of wireless networks using infrared (requires clear line of site) or radio frequency devices.

Tip Number 12. Establish network protocols. Linking machines together provides tremendous advantages but also adds tremendous complexity. Security measures need to be considered. There are a number of important and sometimes very sensitive questions to answer. Will people be allowed to access files on other people's computers? Which ones? Will certain information have restricted access (legal information, payroll records, health information, personal e-mail, etc.)? If so, how will it be protected? How will the team members coordinate their work on shared files so that one team member doesn't accidentally erase the work of someone else when they save their modified version of the document on the server (more on this topic in Chapter 19, "Using Web Tools: Effective Shared Workplaces and Files")? Who is responsible for keeping network software up-to-date? How can viruses be isolated before they spread to the whole network? Should the server be connected to the Internet or isolated from it? Can people put whatever personal software they want on a network-connected computer?

Tip Number 13. Consider the trade-offs between portable versus desktop computers. Desktop computers are less expensive than portables with the same capabilities, but paying the premium for portables is worth it if team members are more productive when they have a computer with them on the road. If they have projects/reports they need to complete while away, need remote access to e-mail or the server, require the ability to make a computer-hosted presentation, or to show a customer your extranet, they'll need some sort of portable. Now that longer battery life, increased memory, and larger screens are available in the portable models, certain kinds of usability problems are not as critical as they once were. The big remaining issues with current portables have more to do with user comfort (i.e., weight of the computer, etc.) than effectiveness. If you do buy portables, have the modems built in. Carrying any more equipment than necessary is not only inconvenient for the traveler, it is one more interface component that can go bad on the road.

Team members who don't need the full functionality of a laptop may have their needs met with a PDA palmtop enabled with their calendar, customer database, and access to e-mail. They often prefer this because of the lower weight.

Tip Number 14. Get access to intranet and Internet services. You'll need both intranet and Internet service to stay connected to employees.

Internet services are required for Web conferences, most e-mail systems, low-cost videoconferencing, professional networking, research, and a whole host of other knowledge transfer opportunities.

Your intranet might be something as simple as an internally shared Web page with information everyone needs on it. Or it might include regularly updated announcements, pricing and/or key financial data, customer information, product information, employee chat rooms, and so forth.

If you want team members to be able to access the intranet from home or from the road, or if you are located at a remote site from where the intranet is hosted, you'll have to set up remote access capability. Although this is fairly easy to do, there are security implications to having this arrangement. If you do want remote access capability, set up a firewall (a combination of hardware [something like a router] and software [including some sort of password checker]) that provide protection from hackers who might be thrilled to have this information from your company. The firewall is especially important if you have a broadband connection to the Internet. In this case the Internet connection will be open all the time to facilitate employee communication with the outside world. Unlike other limited access options, broadband connections like DSL or cable provide a wide window of opportunity for real-time intrusion. Be prepared.

Tip Number 15. Get the peripherals you need. There are a number of other pieces of equipment that virtual offices require, depending on specific user needs. Most offices have a good printer for every few people and some sort of automatic backup system for their server. You'll want at least one printer per office location. Depending on your needs you may also want digital camera and video equipment for training and electronic meetings, scanners to digitize pictures and artwork, electronically enabled whiteboards or graphic tablets that transfer whatever is written on them (project plans, diagrams, schematics, etc.) to the computer network, or a wide variety of other input, storage, or creative resources.

Tip Number 16. Use your Web page for knowledge transfer. Every team can benefit from a Web space where team members can share the tacit knowledge (stuff they know from experience but probably wouldn't be found in a manual anywhere) that is critical to effective virtual teaming.

For example, team start-up Web pages in Arco follow a consistent format. A template has been developed that includes a section for listing learnings from projects, best practices from benchmarking activities, meeting minutes, agendas for upcoming meetings, and links to important Internet sites. After the team starts up they create a home page using another template. This template includes a mandatory link to a company intranet site so that anyone can access any home page (they call them TECHLINKS, the name of virtual teams at Arco). The Arco technologies they are working with are listed across the top of the home page, and the template includes pages for people involved on the team, tools and applications, significant accomplishments, and a chat room section with news and information. Let's review how to set up a Web-site-based knowledge transfer system in more detail.

Creating a Web-Site-Based Knowledge Transfer System

You may want to have a place on your team Web site for shared files, work tools/resources, news, and some sort of chat room to allow team members a place to engage in either synchronous or asynchronous on-line conversations. Distance workers benefit from on-line communications that go beyond e-mail. But use strategy as your guide to appropriate content.

How will you know if you're being strategic? If you spend a lot of time focusing on what your Web site *could* do rather than on what it *should* do to meet business requirements, you may be heading down the wrong road. Avoid the temptation to load it up with nice-to-haves that will waste time, space, and resources. Focus on function, not flash. Spinning icons and overuse of video, 3D graphics, or other memory-hogging elements may make the Web page take so long to load or search that people will avoid using it. Simple is better. It is easy to forget that almost everything that goes on a Web site will require updating and maintenance—a job that will likely fall on your busy distance work team members since it is too big of a job for IT professionals to monitor and support all team sites.

Organize Web page information in the way that makes the most sense to the users. Most knowledge transfer systems that are underutilized suffer from a common problem: The information was organized in a way that made sense to the developer, but not to the user. Some distance leaders try to overorganize their site. Paul McKinnon, senior HR executive at Dell Computers, the $25 billion corporation that is the world's leading direct sales computer company, says that trying to organize everything is ultimately a futile and perhaps even counterproductive activity. He compares it to being the ranger of a large national park who attempts to organize the park by moving all of the waterfalls into one section. "What's important," he says, "is access."[1] People need to know how to get the information they need. Focusing on providing maps is more useful that trying to force-fit incoming information into some type of overly complicated organizational algorithm.

Remember to encourage and reward employee contributions to the knowledge transfer system. Andersen Consulting discovered early on that for these systems to be successful, team members must actually use them. Essential to their competitive strategy, the Andersen intranet provides a way to link 65,000 worldwide employees together and share learnings about industries and consulting projects. Andersen confirms that the key to its success is not the 100 full-time knowledge managers, the physical network of thousands of computers linked to over 300 servers, nor the $500 million annual budget put in place to administer the system. The key is that people actually use it.

Why do they use it? For two reasons: (1) they are *expected* to use it, and (2) the intranet contains valuable information that they can actually apply to their work. Consultants are rewarded for writing white papers and posting them. Andersen employees are well aware that you cannot be promoted if you aren't seen as someone who actively contributes to the system. They also measure the number of hits each white paper receives. Those who write the papers with the most hits are acknowledged in their performance reviews.

In another example of knowledge transfer system reinforcement, Dell CEO Michael Dell announced that he will no longer read e-mail attachments. Instead, Dell e-mails include a URL reference (or hotlink) to the company intranet. This forces people to post information where it is readily accessible to any of the 40,000 employees in the rapidly growing company. This is especially important for Dell, because as of this writing two-thirds of the company's employees have been with Dell less than three years. How are they going to learn the business without access to fast, accurate, and timely information? To ensure the latter, intranet postings have a "freshness dating" like foods in the grocery store. If a posting contains time-sensitive information, it will be tossed as soon as it's stale. While both the Anderson example and the Dell example of knowledge transfer systems are much larger in scope than what most distance leaders will use for their teams, the learning is still very important—you need to reinforce the use of your knowledge transfer system if it is going to be effective.

Tip Number 17. Use the same e-mail program for everyone. Select the e-mail system that best meets your needs. Then stick with it until you all change again. Most browsers have built-in e-mail; it is available through Internet service providers (ISPs), can be downloaded from the Web, purchased through third parties, or developed internally. See Chapter 18, "Management by E-mail—Without Letting It Take Over Your Life," for more information about what many virtual team members consider to be both the biggest blessing and the biggest curse of the modern communication tools.

Tip Number 18. Use Web videoconferencing when it's helpful. If regular videoconferencing is part of your communication practice, you may want to invest in a sophisticated setup such as those described in Chapter 17, "Videoconferencing: Technology and Table Manners." However, the quality of Web videoconferencing with broadband and video compression technologies is rapidly meeting those standards. Consider Web video for its cost-effectiveness and wide availability. All you'll need is digital video cameras for each computer and the software necessary to run the conferencing program you've selected.

However, not all distance managers find Web videoconference useful at the current time. You don't need video just to show a single talking head in a training class, for example. Current Web video is also too slow if you want to replicate reality. Says Mark Armentrout. "The human eye sees about 30 frames a second, while current Web videoconferencing is still between 6 and 15 frames per second. But people who really need to see each other don't complain."

Summary

Although communication technology alone is not enough for distance teams to be successful, it is necessary in order for them to succeed. At a minimum, people need phones with voice mail and computers with e-mail systems. There must be support for teleconferencing and computer networking (including Internet and intranet access). A knowledge transfer system will help team members stay in touch with and learn from each other. Most distance leaders also find other technologies useful. Many find some form of videoconferencing helpful and recommend broadband access to the Internet to increase the speed and effectiveness of data transmission. But ultimately, it is *how* you use what hardware and lines you choose that determines whether the learning transfer and coordination occurs that is so essential to distance work.

Reference

1. From a presentation at the Brigham Young University Organizational Behavior Conference, Provo, Utah, March 31, 2000.

How to Use the Telephone

We try to build relationships with our customers, and having a cell phone makes the account managers more accessible. It's worth the investment.[1]

Shawn Connors, Sales and Marketing Manager
Mesa Sprinklers

IN SPITE OF all the fancy technology at our disposal today, the telephone remains the major form of communication for those working across time and space. And with the advent of the cell phone, we can contact almost anyone from anywhere, any time of the day or night—often in countries that don't yet even have a dependable landline telephone infrastructure.

The telephone is such a familiar part of our daily life, however, that we sometimes take it for granted or view it as a necessary evil that hinders our ability to get "real" work accomplished. Perhaps a few suggestions can help us better utilize the telephone as a primary means of communication with our virtually accessible colleagues.

Tips for Effective Telecommunications

Tip Number 1. Give everyone a cell phone and/or pager. Being able to contact one another quickly and easily, especially at peak or critical points in a project or activity, can save hours of time and prevent miscommunication. Most businesses that have operated virtually for any significant amount of time find that cellular technology can be a lifesaver. Most acknowledge that the advantages of having each individual accessible far outweigh other considerations such as cost. Some organizations, such as Xerox, have found that a combination of pagers, voice mail, and cell phones helps keep everyone on top of the many changes that businesses face day-to-day. "We use a pager system that is tied to our voice-mail system," says Martin O'Connor, manager of property management east, Xerox Corporation. "If you leave us a [message], the voice mail system calls our pager and relays the message. We use our cell phones to return those calls."[2]

There are methods, including various calling plans and tracking features, that help to manage the costs associated with cellular technology. Tracking features such as that described by Jim Gerace, a spokesperson for Bell Atlantic Mobile in Bedminster, New Jersey, can also help monitor costs. He recommends that small companies on tight budgets purchase timers that appear on each unit so that users can monitor their phone use more carefully. This also allows managers to assess which individuals are accumulating the most phone time.[3] Local service providers can help determine which of the current plans or other methods would best serve your needs. Appropriateness depends on a variety of factors such as company size, group size, number of locations, and so forth.

Tip Number 2. Never implement Tip Number One without immediately following up with Tip Number Three.

Tip Number 3. Establish agreements about cell phone and pager use. Just because it is technologically possible to contact someone at any time doesn't mean that it is a good idea to do so. Everyone needs personal and family time. And having cell phones going off during meetings, while talking on desk phones, or while having a whiteboard or other cyberspace meeting is very distracting to others.

The phone/pager discussion can include setting some boundaries about usage and cost. Setting expectations and getting agreement up front eliminates abuse or misunderstandings later.

Tip Number 4. When tethered to a desk phone, use a headset. As discussed in other chapters, teleconferences are a big part of working across distance. So is one-on-one phone time. As the authors can attest (having spent many hours consulting via telephone), you can destroy your neck by cradling a phone for long periods. Carrying on a lengthy conversation while taking notes, looking through papers and other materials, or working on a computer whiteboard calls for ergonomically sound measures. Using a headset frees you up to work the computer, jot down key points, or even talk more normally by using your hands, if that's your style!

Don't assume that just any headset will do. You may have to try out a few different models or types. We found, for instance, that when used in conjunction with our phone system, some headsets made us sound tinny or like we were in a deep well. Only purchase a headset from a dealer who will let you return it if it doesn't meet your need. While testing different options, be sure to call your colleagues who are located in distant offices and let them give you feedback on the quality of sound. You usually don't even have to ask. If you sound like you fell in a well, they will almost certainly mention that as soon as you say "Hello." If they are pleasantly surprised to learn that you are talking into a headset instead of the receiver, that is a good sign.

One caution: Most headsets have a handle that affixes to the handset and is used to dislodge it from its cradle to make a call or to answer incoming calls. It works in such as way that you don't actually remove the handset from the phone cradle. Therefore, it is sometimes easy to remove the headset when the conversation is over but forget to actually sever the connection. Remember to push that handle down when you finish the conversation. Otherwise, the party you were speaking with may hear your follow-up comments, or you and your coworkers in surrounding offices or cubicles will hear that annoying signal that lets you know the phone is off the hook.

Tip Number 5. Demonstrate phone courtesy. Almost all issues associated with management or communication get amplified when managing from a distance. This is true of phone manners, too. Here are a few phone etiquette reminders:

1. Pay attention to the conversation. Distance managers are often required to spend extraordinary amounts of time on the phone in lengthy, detailed, potentially boring conversations. This can result in "management drift"—that process of reflecting on issues other than the one being discussed. We are usually most susceptive to this during teleconferences where more than two people are participating. It is easy to assume, consciously or unconsciously, that others will stay tuned in and that your own wanderings won't be noticed. But it's easy to get caught short when someone directs a question at you or asks your opinion on the topic at hand.

2. Be sensitive to voice volume. Keep your voice low enough so that those in the surrounding office area aren't disturbed, but loud enough so that those on the line can clearly hear you.

3. Avoid talking over others. This tends to happen more frequently in phone conversations because we don't have the advantage of body language to clue us that the other individual is getting ready to speak. If you do cut others off, apologize and offer to let them complete their thought.

4. When calling unannounced, ask the person if this is a good time to talk; don't assume that they are free to take the call right now. For longer conversations, schedule ahead of time just as you would for a face-to-face meeting.

5. Return phone calls in a timely way. If your virtual team has operating guidelines outlining what "timely" means, honor those guidelines.

6. Minimize interruptions. Find a way to let others in your office know that you are on the phone and can't be disturbed. One way to do this is to post a sign on your office door or cubicle entrance that tells people you are on the phone and can't be disturbed. Include a space on the sign for people to leave messages, or hang a sticky pad by the sign so they can jot you a note. This lets you know who came by so you can follow up with them when the call is finished. All of this may sound crazy, but remember, if you are using a headset other people can't necessarily tell that you are on the phone. Frequently we have been in the middle of a telephone conversation when a team member walked into the office

and began talking because he or she didn't see the telltale handset clasped to our ear.

Tip Number 6. Respect time zones. When working with individuals from multiple time zones, establish protocols about appropriate times to call. Make sure that everyone gets the opportunity to get up in the middle of the night for teleconferences, rather than limiting that to a few poor souls in the hinterlands.

Also respect people's personal time. Try to avoid frequently scheduling calls that require individuals to come in early or stay well past the close of their workday. While this is to be expected occasionally, doing so on a regular or frequent basis can burn people out.

Tip Number 7. Use printed information to increase clarity. Computer whiteboard technology may eventually render this a moot point. In the meantime, however, if that technology isn't available to all parties, a complex conversation is greatly enhanced via the use of pictures, diagrams, or other printed materials. A discussion regarding a parts problem, for instance, is much more effective if all those in the conversation have a drawing of the part. Send any written information ahead of time to reduce questions or confusion or simply to ensure a richer discussion. We have a client who regularly sends a fax with any reference information just prior to a scheduled telephone call. It really helps.

Be sure that all written documents have page numbers. Referencing a page number is much easier than trying to describe which page you are on and then waiting for others to catch up.

Tip Number 8. Utilize visual imagery. As all of us know, the lack of visual clues can be a major hindrance to phone interaction. This is especially problematic when the conversation involves multiple parties. One virtual team at Hewlett-Packard created their own phone meeting language to compensate for not being able to see one another. Says HP consultant Peter Bartlett, "I found myself saying things like, 'John, I assume you are nodding now,' or asking, 'Mary, are you rolling your eyes?' to make these behaviors visible on the phone."[4]

The client we mentioned in the previous tip is also very good at using visual imagery in a different way. While describing a complex training model she once stopped and said, "Imagine a two-dimensional box divided into four parts. The axis on the left side is complexity, ranging from low on the bottom to high on the top. The axis on the bottom of the square is time, ranging from short-term on the left to long-term on the right." The author drew the box on a pad in front of him. When the conversation resumed and the client explained how the approach would be different depending on which quadrant we were discussing (high complexity short-term; high complexity long-term; low complexity short-term; or low complexity long-term), the author simply referenced the diagram he had drawn according to her visually oriented instructions. The diagram description had added a little more time up front, but it made the conversation much more intelligible.

Tip Number 9. Set protocols for voice mail use. Although e-mail is fast becoming the corporate communication tool of choice, voice mail still has a vital place in virtual communication. Voice mail has the advantage of conveying the sender's tone of voice, which adds another important dimension to telecommunication. But like e-mail, voice mail usage can run amok. Just as we suggest setting protocols for e-mail use (see Chapter 18, "Management by E-mail—Without Letting It Take Over Your Life"), we also suggest use agreements for voice mail. See Figure 15.1 for examples of voice mail protocols. These can be developed as part of the operating guidelines discussion described in Chapter 6, "Distance Team Building: Practical Tips for Building Effective Teams."

- We check our voice mail at least once a day.
- We use the "urgent" code only when a message is truly urgent.
- We limit use of the "group send" option. We use it only when a message is relevant to all members.
- When forwarding messages we will leave an explanatory message so the individual knows why the message is being sent.
- We take accountability to follow up voice mail messages with written documentation when necessary.
- We never use voice mail to leave emotionally charged messages. We wait to talk with the person directly so the problem or issue can be jointly resolved.

Figure 15.1   Voice Mail Protocol Examples

In order to set these protocols, it is useful for the virtual team to answer a few questions pertaining to this technology. These questions include:

- What will we use voice mail for?
- What will we not use it for?
- How frequently will we leave voice messages?
- Will we need to check voice mail on weekends, holidays, and vacations?
- How quickly will we commit to responding to messages?
- Do we need to create a way to designate message priorities (urgent, FYI, etc.)?
- When will we transfer messages from one voice mail box to another?
- Is there any special protocol for transfers (can we just transfer, or do we need to leave an explanatory message)?[5]

Finally, respect others' voice mail time. Avoid leaving very lengthy or detailed messages. Instead, briefly explain the nature of the call or issue and request that the individual call you back to discuss the details.

Tip Number 10. As previously mentioned, avoid using the telephone to address performance issues. Whenever possible, performance issues are best dealt with face-to-face (see Chapter 12, "The Necessity of Face-to-Face Meetings"). These are often emotion-filled conversations that require the utmost clarity. Being face-to-face facilitates greater understanding and resolution of problem(s).

In emergencies where the situation doesn't allow travel time, you might have to fax documentation to the other person to facilitate increased understanding and to ensure that key points are received. Then follow up with regular coaching sessions to ensure that every measure is taken to create a successful outcome.

Summary

The telephone still remains one of the quickest, easiest, and most user-friendly forms of communication. Its use in business is so pervasive that we recommend that those who are working virtually be provided with cellular technology to ensure fast, accurate transfer of information. In order to avoid some of the common problems of overuse or abuse, we also suggest that virtual groups establish protocols and boundaries for use of cellular technology.

Other ways to more effectively use telephone technology include using headsets when working from a desk phone, establishing voice mail protocols, enhancing conversations with printed materials, employing visual imagery to avoid missing out on visual communication cues, and respecting time zones. We also advise against using the telephone to address performance issues whenever doing so can be avoided, and suggest using printed material in conjunction with the conversation when it cannot. Finally, demonstrating basic phone courtesy can make telephone conversations more pleasant and tolerable, rather than a necessary irritant.

References

1. Tricia Campbell, "Are Cellular Phones Worth the Price?" *Sales and Marketing Management,* November 1997, p. 97.
2. Clara Vangen, "Communications and Technology, Special Report: Technology Today & Tomorrow," *Buildings,* December 1998, p. 37.
3. Tricia Campbell, "Are Cellular Phones Worth the Price?," *Sales and Marketing Management,* November 1997, p. 97.
4. Kimball Fisher and Mareen Duncan Fisher, *The Distributed Mind,* AMACOM, 1998, p. 257.
5. Ibid.

The Distance Manager's Guide to Efficient Teleconferences

Virtual meetings require that the manager or sponsor of the meeting is more organized than normal. They have to have their act together. They have to think about meeting preparation more than usual.

Lynn Buchanan,
Internal Strategic Education Consultant
Weyerhaeuser Company

TELECONFERENCING HAS BECOME an almost universal method of communication in the conducting of business. Often those who are participants in teleconferences complain that it just doesn't seem to get the job done as well as face-to-face meetings. But Lynn Buchanan, Strategic Education Consultant at Weyerhaeuser Company, who has seen a distinct rise in the use of teleconferencing over the last

3 years, enthusiastically expounds on the advantages this mode of communication provides. "It saves time and money. It leaves me with more discretionary time—I don't have to get on an airplane to conduct business." Buchanan points out that there may even be advantages to using teleconferencing when participants are nearby. Weyerhaeuser's headquarters facilities, for instance, are spread throughout Federal Way and Tacoma, Washington. Buchanan recounts various occasions when having a teleconference saved her and several others the 45-plus minutes in travel and set-up time that would be needed for a face-to-face meeting in the headquarters region. But, as Buchanan and many other managers are learning, a teleconference alone won't necessarily save time if certain protocols aren't followed. Here are tips from Buchanan and others who have found that teleconferencing technology can dramatically improve their productivity.

Tips for Teleconferencing

Tip Number 1. Get organized! Teleconferences can't be conducted "on the fly" or without considerable forethought and planning. Those who use teleconferences regularly and successfully will testify that these meetings require greater amounts of preparation than a face-to-face session. The rules we all know about how to ensure an effective meeting need to be followed with particular care when teleconferencing. Have an agenda and send it out to all teleconference participants in advance of the call. This allows those involved to come prepared with whatever information, research, and documents, they need to fully contribute. Keeping attention focused in a remote conversation is difficult at best. Having participants checking out to run to their desks to retrieve materials or information only exacerbates the situation.

Tip Number 2. Assign meeting roles. Another key to organizing teleconferences for optimal payout is to assign each participant a role to play throughout the session.

Helpful roles include what Buchanan calls being a *phone leader.* The role of the phone leader is to ensure that everyone has equal opportunity to speak. As Buchanan points out, in a face-to-face meeting, "body language often serves to clue participants that someone wishes to speak. Without that visibility, member contributions can get lost. Quieter individuals may give up trying to get into the conversation."

One phone leader Buchanan worked with actually kept a list of participants' names in front of him. During a video-supported teleconference session, as each member spoke the phone leader would place a check by the individual's name so that he could track participation and solicit input from those who hadn't had an opportunity yet to be heard. This is especially important in teleconferences where you don't have the additional advantage of video.

Most teams find it useful to rotate the meeting role(s) so that these types of responsibilities are shared. Whatever you choose to call them, consider assigning these four important roles for each meeting:

- *Scribe.* The scribe keeps notes for the meeting and distributes them afterward. He or she pays special attention to key decisions made, important information shared, and action items that need to be followed up on.
- *Gatekeeper.* The gatekeeper watches the gate of participation and opens it to those who haven't participated much, while closing it to those who have had a disproportionate amount of talk time. (The gatekeeper might say something like, "Thanks for your input, Jane. Mary, what are *your* concerns?") The phone leader previously mentioned is a type of gatekeeper.
- *Leader.* The leader organizes the meeting and facilitates it. Although distance managers often play this role themselves, rotating this assignment gives other team members a chance to learn leadership skills and share in the management roles and responsibilities. Typically the leader keeps the group on track by assuring that the most important parts of the agenda are covered in the allotted time.
- *Participant.* Although it may seem that being a participant isn't a specific meeting role, effective groups soon discover that everyone in the meeting has certain responsibilities, such as supporting group decisions, honestly expressing their views, sticking to the agenda, and respecting others. Having these types of expectations clarified prior to teleconferencing makes it more effective and efficient.

Tip Number 3. Use people's names. When you cannot see the meeting participants, it is sometimes difficult to know who is speaking. This can result in confusion both in the conversation and afterwards, when people are unclear about who said what or who took which assignments. It also makes it much easier for the scribe or note taker to identify assignments and to accurately capture the meeting proceedings. At the start of the meeting, have the members at each site introduce themselves, then set the guideline that each individual will identify her- or himself each time they speak. Likewise, when responding to someone else's comment or question, use their name. This degree of discipline will keep the meeting clear and on track.

This is sometimes more difficult to do, however, when some of the people in the meeting are co-located while others participate remotely. For example, one of this book's authors recently participated in a series of teleconferences when a client was conducting interviews of their customers. They set up a number of focus groups which included some customers who appeared in person as well as a number of other customers (about one-third of the participants) who joined the interview by telephone. A high-quality teleconference system with multiple microphones was set up to accommodate the meeting. At the beginning of each focus group session, the leader asked each person to introduce him- or herself and made sure that everyone could hear everyone else. He then reviewed the agenda that had been sent to each of the 80 or so participants beforehand. The gatekeeper then explained a number of ground rules that the team had developed in order to make the best use of the teleconference, including a request to begin each comment with the name of the person speaking.

Although the remote participants were pretty good at remembering to use their names, the author noticed that when there was a larger group of on-site participants than remote ones, it was easy for the on-site people to forget to begin their comments with their name. The gatekeeper did two things to help overcome this problem.

First, he followed an unintroduced statement with something like, "For the benefit of those of you who couldn't recognize her voice, that was Mary," or, "That comment was from Pete." After four or five times of doing that, the participants would normally get back into the habit of beginning their comments by saying something like, "This is Pete and I have to disagree with that last comment from Mary."

The second thing the gatekeeper did was to have name tents made up for each participant whether they were on-site or not. Having a name tent at an open chair for each of the off-site participants made it easier to remember that there were other people in the meeting who needed to be included and who didn't have the advantage of being within viewing distance of the speakers. Participants later reported that this was a helpful reminder.

Tip Number 4. Remember that silence is not consent. The leader can perform a very helpful service by checking with each individual when decisions are made, to determine whether they are in agreement and will support the implementation and outcome of the decision. Without visual stimulation to keep participants engaged and alert, it is easy to check out or to abdicate ownership for decisions the group solves. Make sure that every person voices his or her concerns before closing on a decision.

Tip Number 5. Remember to use the tips introduced in Chapter 15, "How to Use the Telephone." Visual cues, in particular, can be very helpful. As mentioned in that chapter, one Hewlett-Packard operation found that they could communicate more effectively by stating what they assumed people were doing but which they could not see for themselves. They would ask, "Marion, are you shaking your head and wincing right now?" or, "Bill, are you smiling at that last comment?" rather than have unconfirmed pictures like this in their minds. An even more direct application of this tip is to have people articulate the things they see themselves or others doing that are invisible to distant team members. You might say, "I'm holding up that report we did last month because I'm afraid we've already forgotten it," or, "You guys should see Lee right now; she's holding her hands around her throat like she's choking."

Tip Number 6. Provide training and preparation in the effective use of teleconferencing. As with any other technology, teleconferencing requires that people be properly prepared in order to make the best use of it. Teach participants both the technical (e.g., how to join the conference or add someone in) and the social skills necessary to complete the conferences successfully. Both types of skills are important. Don't assume that if someone knows how to use a telephone they will make effective use of teleconferencing.

As we have mentioned in previous chapters, one especially important social skill is basic courtesy. "Manners prevail whenever you are communicating via technology rather than in person," Buchanan reminds us. "Rudeness is magnified tenfold when you aren't face-to-face." In order to avoid distracting or inappropriate behaviors, have some communication guidelines sent to participants prior to the meeting. These can include tips such as being on time for the call, using each other's names (see Tip Number Three in this section), not talking over one another, not conducting sidebar conversations with people at your site while others are talking from other sites, staying alert and paying attention, and not rifling through papers that are located next to the speaker phone.

Tip Number 7. Be especially careful about background sounds over the phone. In the customer panel teleconferences just mentioned, some of the participants apparently didn't realize how well ambient noise can travel over the phone. From time to time we heard music (a nearby radio?), nose-blowing, throat clearing, eating noises, and even periodic background conversations (from passersby?). In a later teleconference, when we were discussing the customer data collected by the interviews, a remote participant who was joining us from her hotel room made screeching noises from moving her chair that were so loud that the other participants had to tell her to use the mute button unless she was talking. Some Web conference programs now allow the instructor/coordinator to remotely mute the audio portion of the conference for a distracted participant who doesn't realize the noises he or she is making. It's difficult enough to use these technologies without having to battle with avoidable distractions.

Summary

Observing a few practical tips on teleconferencing can have a tremendous impact on the effectiveness and efficiency of this common communication technology. Team members and distance leaders alike benefit from a few specific technical and social teleconferencing skills. In particular, provide training, use visual cues, reduce background noise, and remember that silence is not consent. Use names, assign meeting roles, and get organized for teleconferences to improve the effectiveness of this important tool.

Videoconferencing: Technology and Table Manners

Use videoconferencing for what it was intended for. Don't just use it for watching each other in meeting rooms or at your PC. The true power of videoconferencing isn't realized until you get the camera out into the field and say, "Hey, this is a picture of the construction site; look at how far we've come since last week," or, "Watch what happens on the video screen when we start up this piece of equipment; maybe if we all look at it we can figure out what's wrong."

Mark Armentrout, Manager of Information Technology
Arco Exploration and Production

V IDEOCONFERENCING HAS ARRIVED. Once only a fantasy product at Disneyland, this technology has finally improved to the point where fairly high-quality products are available at reasonable prices. Even a basic system used to cost $25,000 per videoconference room, plus the cost of using multiple Integrated Services Digital Network (ISDN) telephone lines to ensure good video and audio quality. But set-top (smaller integrated units that connect to a monitor) prices are falling to just a few thousand dollars each and can often be cost-justified by the travel savings associated with eliminating just a couple of trips. Using desktop videoconferencing over the Internet is even more reasonable, with software and cameras costing only hundreds of dollars per workstation. Although these Web-based systems are still relatively primitive, recent advances in compression technology that allow fairly good video over low bandwidth connections offer great promise for the near future.

Consider some examples of the benefits of video communication. Xerox scientists in Portland, Oregon, and Palo Alto, California, arranged for a constantly open phone line, computer linking, and videoconferencing between the two offices. They would simply walk up to a camera set up in a conference room in each location and start talking to colleagues as though the video meeting room was another office space. Remote scientists would hear them call out and come in to *their* video conference room to talk. With the aid of these technologies, they found that being in separate locations was not a significant barrier to collaboration.[1]

Although law firms often tend to be more conservative in applying advanced communication technologies than large corporations or high-tech industries might, many of them are on the videoconference wagon as well. For example, Sutherland, Asbill and Brennan, a law firm with 250 lawyers (575 total employees) divided between offices in Washington, D.C., and Atlanta, Georgia, has used videoconferencing since 1997. Benefits of the system include the ability to "see facial expressions and reactions that can be hidden on the phone."[2] Reebok, the sports apparel company, used videoconferencing to great advantage to facilitate communication across the globe when their MIS team needed a way to implement an enterprise resource planning (ERP) system. The New York State Teachers' Retirement System administers retirement benefits for over 93,000 public school teachers and administrators. Their use of videoconferencing improved customer service, saved money, and improved information transfer. In one survey, 90 percent of people who participated in the testing of the new system said that when computer links were added to the videoconference, "a video consultation was as good or better than a face-to-face meeting."[3]

The Challenges of Videoconferencing

There are still considerable challenges associated with this communication methodology. Not long ago, the authors had a videoconference with a large *Fortune* 100 company. Participants included representatives from four different sites in addition to us and some staff members at the company corporate headquarters location. The conference started well. There were video pictures from each of the remote sites as the people from the various locations introduced themselves and asked a series of questions to which we responded. The participants were clearly well prepared for the conference, and the meeting was well organized and facilitated by a staff member at the headquarters location.

After the initial question-and-answer period with each site, we made a brief presentation. During our presentation their particular technology automatically rotated the pictures on the monitor so that each site was highlighted in turn. This allowed us to watch the responses of the remote sites during the presentation. When the first three video pictures came onto the screen in turn at the headquarters location, we saw small groups of employees nodding their heads and listening attentively. But the fourth video feed was different. A woman who was the single representative of her organization started eating lunch on camera. When her video came on screen, there were distracting noises as she shuffled and crumpled her plastic and paper bags. She looked at her food instead of at the camera and began vigorously scratching her nose. The facilitator, afraid to embarrass the woman by saying something, remained silent. Although the picture lasted only a few moments, we found it difficult to keep our train of thought.

The Benefits of Using Ears and Eyes

Videoconferencing is to teleconferencing what television is to radio. Although it will never completely displace the ubiquitous telephone, it will become more dominant as a means of communication as world infrastructure and improving technologies facilitate it.

Having the opportunity to use more senses enhances communication. Much of the way we communicate as human beings is nonverbal. When I see you scowling or slowly nodding your head up and down I get more information about your receptiveness to my message than your silence may otherwise indicate. I can often see whether you appear happy or sad, engaged or bored. I can see visual cues that you are confused or that you want to say something. A talented reader of body language can do even more. Although these cues are not always perceived accurately (e.g., a frown may only mean that you're thinking, rather than that you disagree), they provide a whole additional layer of richness to a conversation that helps the communication be much more effective and efficient.

At the time of this writing, many of the video technologies are still rather clumsy. Many of the people we interviewed, for example, complained of long, awkward pauses between the sending and receiving of messages. Some—especially those who used desktop videoconferencing over the Internet—mentioned that the video pictures were so slow (changed frames per second) or had such low resolution that they provided little benefit over a teleconference. Others noted that large group shots made it difficult to see the reactions of specific people or to see who was speaking. Many have actually chosen to not use videoconferencing until these types of problems have cost-effective solutions. But this technology is changing so rapidly that most of these types of problems will soon cease to exist. Videoconferencing is clearly here to stay. So the question is, "How can we make videoconferencing more effective?"

Tips for Videoconferencing

Consider these dozen tips for using videoconferencing:

Tip Number 1. Consult an expert when seeking the most appropriate videoconferencing technology for your organization. Generally speaking, you currently have two primary choices: (1) you can go with an internal conference room system with matched equipment at all sites, or (2) you can use a desktop Internet-based system that works over the Web with a variety of platforms.

We believe that eventually videoconferencing will be done primarily over the Internet. It's cheaper and more accessible than the alternatives. The problem right now, however, is that Internet-based videoconferencing has significantly lower quality than internal conference room systems. It also puts a lot of additional pressure on already crowded local area networks. But this technology is changing very rapidly. It's best to consult with an expert to evaluate the pros and cons before you and your team select the right mix of technology at the level of quality you need and at the prices you can afford. Remember that videoconferencing equipment isn't limited to cameras, monitors, and software. It has to run on your telephone and/or network lines. Some companies even isolate videoconferencing on a separate network for capacity and security reasons.

Choose whatever best meets your needs. Normally you'll need a way for everyone to see three things: (1) remote participants (multiple remotes may require different equipment/software than just two stations do); (2) themselves (to make sure that they are projecting the desired image and to avoid embarrassing moments); and (3) a linked computer screen (for presentations or demonstrations).

Tip Number 2. Know the limits of the technology you choose. Currently, while internal video-room-based systems have better quality, they are more expensive and difficult to interface with different systems (like those used by your vendors or customers). On the other hand, Web systems are currently slow and stilted but require only a good camera and some software to operate almost anywhere. They normally are limited to one person per station and are difficult to use if you want to get small groups together from different locations. Although current technology allows you to see 15 other single-camera sources on your PC screen at one time, it still falls short of achieving the degree of collaboration that can occur when a few people at a site meet together face-to-face.

There are other limits to remember as well. With certain systems you may need to pause after each comment to allow appropriate transmission time and prevent people from continuously cutting each other off. Learn the flow of your technology. You may have to adapt your normal speech and meeting patterns to accommodate it. In one video-conference with a client, for example, one of this book's authors told a joke at the beginning of the session. When the remote site participants didn't laugh, he assumed that they didn't get the joke and so he proceeded to explain it. A few seconds later, however, they started laughing just as he was explaining the joke. Their reaction was caused by transmission delay. It took several minutes before everyone understood how the delay would affect the session. It certainly made humor difficult, since timing is so important to effective joke delivery.

Tip Number 3. Use the applicable tips from the teleconferencing chapter. Like teleconferences, videoconferences require excellent preparation and facilitation. See Chapter 16, "The Distance Manager's Guide to Efficient Teleconferences," for more information on things like getting organized, assigning meeting roles, using names, being polite, and providing training.

Tip Number 4. Remember that you're on camera. Don't do anything on a videoconference that you wouldn't do on live television. As we have already mentioned several times, technology can amplify problems manyfold. Things that might be acceptable in face-to-face meetings (eating, shuffling papers, moving around) can really be problematic in videoconferencing. If the woman in the story that opens this chapter had remembered this tip she would have been able to avoid a very embarrassing moment in front of her peers.

Tip Number 5. Fill up the video frame. Stay close to the camera. Bill Blankenship, a vice president for Weyerhaeuser Company, complains that some people shy away from the camera during videoconferencing, especially if they are using desktop video systems. "Stay close to the camera," he recommends, "Nobody wants to see some miniature face in the corner of the screen."

Tip Number 6. Don't limit yourselves to talking heads. Take advantage of the full potential of this technology. Show video shorts from the company president's last speech. Take a video camera into the field and show someone actually closing a sale with a customer or tearing apart a pump. Don't just talk about it—demonstrate it. Surgeons have been using these kinds of videoconferencing techniques for years as a way to train each other about new techniques and tools. A picture is worth a thousand words—if it's the right picture.

Tip Number 7. Create video use protocols with the team. Define your own set of video table manners. What's OK? What's not OK? These agreements may be different from organization to organization. That's fine as long as the people who must use the technology agree to the protocols.

Tip Number 8. Use the mute feature when you aren't talking. Microphones can be very sensitive. If you are in a portion of a conference where there isn't interactivity, muting your mike can eliminate unnecessary noise. Be very careful, however, of what you say even if you think the mute is on. There are lots of horror stories about things being unintentionally overheard. Play it safe. Don't say anything during a videoconference (mute off or on) that you don't want other people to overhear. This includes the last part of the conference when microphones are still on as people are leaving.

Tip Number 9. Limit your videoconferences to a maximum of two hours. Sometimes the temptation is to use a videoconference in the same way as a face-to-face meeting. But people have to work much harder to concentrate and to participate in videoconferences than in face-to-face meetings. They will tire more rapidly and be less able to be attentive after a shorter time than in physical meetings. In our experience, two hours is the practical limit for a single videoconference. As in all meetings, shorter is better.

Tip Number 10. Give people as much control over the technology as possible. For example, find ways to let them zoom in on a particular person rather than be limited to a static view. Create as much interactivity as possible under the technological constraints you have. When people have more control over the technology, they are more likely to use it effectively.

Tip Number 11. Respect people's privacy. Some employees fear that videoconferencing technologies will be used to monitor their work remotely, like the security systems in retail stores. This fear can create distrust and erode morale. It can also make people avoid using the technology. Don't do things that look like spying on team members.

To allay fears about using video as a Big Brother, respect privacy especially in instances when you are using videoconferencing with home-based workers. Remember that videoconferencing is much more intrusive than teleconferencing and may also require more preparation on the part of the remote party (e.g., getting cleaned up, fixing up the room where the camera is located, making sure the kids are taken care of). Never engage in videoconferences without warning. This will be especially important to remember as technology proceeds to the point that the sender can activate it.

Tip Number 12. Don't use videoconferencing for things you shouldn't use it for. Remember that some things need to be done in person. In addition to things we've already discussed, people we interviewed suggested that a first interaction with a customer and the first interview with a potential new hire normally shouldn't be done over a videoconference.

Summary

Videoconferencing can be one of the most effective technologies for distance communication and training because it engages multiple senses. But employing a few tips can make the difference between effective videoconferences and an irritating waste of time and money. In this chapter we have reviewed several key recommendations, including not using videoconferencing for things it shouldn't be used for, respecting the privacy of others, giving participants as much control as possible over the technology, limiting videoconferences to two hours, using the mute feature when appropriate, creating use protocols, not limiting your meeting to talking heads, filling up the video frame, remembering you're on camera, using applicable teleconferencing tips, knowing the limitations of your technology, and checking with an expert when seeking the appropriate videoconferencing equipment for your application.

References

1. Anthony M. Townsend, Samuel M. DeMarie, and Anthony R. Hendrickson, "Virtual Teams: Technology and the Workplace of the Future," *The Academy of Management Executive,* August 1998, v.12, n3.
2. Melanie D. Goldman, "D.C. Firm Meets on Video with Its Office in Atlanta," *Washington Business Journal,* Feb. 5, 1999, v17, i40.
3. David T. Daly, "Technology for Customer Service: Videoconferencing at the New York State Teachers' Retirement System," *Gov-*

ernment Finance Review, Feb. 1999, v15, i1. Used with permission of the Government Finance Officers Association, publisher of *Government Finance Review,* 180 N. Michigan Ave., Suite 800, Chicago, Illinois, USA, 60601, phone (312) 977-9700, fax (312) 977-4806, e-mail GFR@gfoa.org, Web site www.gfoa.org. Annual subscriptions: $30.00.

Managing by E-mail— Without Letting It Take Over Your Life

I'd love to be a barrier buster, and a business analyzer, and coach my employees. But I get 75 e-mails a day! That's all I have time for!

Anonymous Operations Manager
Southern Natural Gas

INFORMATION TECHNOLOGY IS a two-edged sword. The availability of so much information can cause overload and frustration on the part of many leaders. Therefore, finding ways to manage information in a way that allows the distance manager and his or her virtual team(s) to have all the information they need to be effective—without having more than is necessary—is vital.

A technology that is a mixed blessing in this regard is e-mail. In one training class not long ago, we heard a manager complain that his ability to be a leader was negatively affected by e-mail glut. The time he might have spent doing the things he knew would make him a more effective leader was often being used up with reading and responding to e-mail.

Unfortunately, this is hardly unusual anymore. We learned of one engineer at Hewlett-Packard, for example, who came back from vacation to find more than 200 lengthy e-mails waiting for him. He was already time-starved because of his need to catch up on things that happened on his project while he was gone. When asked what he did with the e-mails when he returned, he informed the interviewer that he quickly deleted every one of them. "If they're important, people will resend them," he said. It's sad when someone can't even take the time to screen e-mail for critical data. When we told this story to some of our friends at Intel, they were amazed. We were interested, however, in what they were amazed at. "Wow!" they would typically say with some envy in their voices, "How come he only had 200 e-mails!"

In this chapter we will review tips for managing the avalanche of data that many distance managers and virtual teams receive via e-mail. We'll discuss establishing protocols for the leader and team members that will facilitate better e-mail management. We will also consider several other things relative to this technology that distance managers should be aware of, including tips for dealing with spam (unsolicited e-mail), general organizational tips, suggestions about dealing with sensitive issues such as humor and confidential information, and some legal issues associated with e-mail management.

Tips for Reducing E-mail Glut

We'll start with a number of tips about how to reduce e-mail overload. Some of these tips require group discussion and training. Some of these tips also require you to use certain features in your e-mail program. The way you do it may differ or not be available depending on the program you have, but we have tried to make suggestions that most popular programs support. Remember to also use your own interactions with the team to set an example for proper e-mail use.

Tip Number 1. Have a "no-scrolling" rule. Procter & Gamble has long-employed the one-page rule for written memos. If you send a memo that is longer than one page, only the first page is read. That forces everyone to make their communication clear and succinct, and to put the most important information right up front. A number of companies use a similar rule for e-mail—"If it's more than a screen page in length, it's too long." If you have to scroll down to read an e-mail, it is probably something that should be discussed in another venue (e.g., face-to-face, voice mail) or it is including information that should probably be sent as an attachment or separate e-mail. There may, of course, be exceptions to this rule, but several distance managers confirmed that "no scrolling" is a very important discipline to maintain. Messages that are brief and tightly focused save time for both the sender and the recipient.

Tip Number 2. Avoid group replies. As one manager in Pioneer Hi-Bred, International aptly put it: "The single biggest improvement we could make in this company to increase productivity would be to disable the group reply button on e-mail!" Using group replies requires an enormous amount of time on the part of the receiver to scroll through the mailing list just to find the message. Using group reply means that countless numbers of people receive copies of documents they may not need, thus clogging the e-mail system with useless information. Or, even more irritating, numerous individuals sometimes even get caught in a written debate in which they have little interest. While there are valid reasons to use a group reply feature it should be assiduously avoided when possible.

Tip Number 3. Keep group lists up to date. In a related tip, if you do have to use group replies, make sure that the lists are always current. Sending an e-mail to someone who is no longer on the project team is akin to spamming.

Tip Number 4. Don't leave everyone's attachments or full dialogue on e-mail replies. In those running message types of e-mails that get circulated around from time to time, don't just add comments and then send it on unmodified. Quote only the portions from previous messages that have relevance. If the attachment is no longer useful, delete it. Imagine how much time could be saved if the e-mail world took this counsel to heart. Spending a minimum amount of time on the sending end can save cumulative hours on the receiving end.

Tip Number 5. Check e-mail regularly. This prevents a pile-up of messages and eliminates the tedium associated with reading through thirty or forty messages at a sitting.

Obviously, there are many issues that can be handled effectively via e-mail if they are addressed in a timely manner. If not addressed quickly, however, some issues escalate into an ordeal that requires phone calls, teleconferences, video meetings or face-to-face meetings, which can also mean travel time.

Tip Number 6. Use the description line well. This allows people to determine the urgency and relevance of an e-mail. Some operations establish a coding system that helps people determine whether something requires immediate attention or not. If you do this be careful about using obvious words like "urgent." This and certain other words are being used more frequently by spammers in an attempt to get people to read their e-mails.

Tip Number 7. Use automatic replies when necessary. When you're on vacation or can't reply to e-mails for a while, use automatic replies to let everyone who sends you an e-mail during that period know that you won't be able to reply until you get back. This helps people understand why you let their e-mail sit around for a few days, and discourages them from flooding your in-box with additional messages.

Tip Number 8. Establish electronic communication protocols as a team. Consider the types of tips suggested in this chapter, along with your company's corporate guidelines or mandates relative to e-mail use, and then establish team agreements. Knowledge transfer protocols such as those in Figure 18.1 can be an effective technique for improving the use and control of e-mail. Protocols help people agree on how to avoid clogging the system.

When establishing such protocols, keep in mind that e-mail is most helpful for (1) general, nonurgent materials where it is useful to (2) retain documentation, (3) interaction is not required, and (4) security is not important. For instance, one protocol might state that if a message is truly important, it gets communicated face-to-face or voice-to-voice. Or, if it consists of specific material useful to only a few members on the team, then only those people get it. Having a few well-thought-out agreements such as these can go a long way in eliminating the negative effects of e-mail.

Spam Tips

Tip Number 9. Have a "no spam" rule. Obviously, using company e-mail to promote personal business is normally inappropriate. But spam is much more than unsolicited advertising. It is anything that is

- We will clearly identify the subject of the message in the subject line.
- All e-mail messages will be short (no scrolling required) and to the point.
- E-mail will not be used for philosophical debates.
- We agree to keep all distribution lists current.
- E-mail won't be used for urgent messages.
- We accept responsibility for a personal delivery (face-to-face or voice-to-voice) of any urgent message.
- To enable message prioritization, we will code the top of each message with either "requires action" or "for your information (FYI)."
- We will sign all messages.
- We agree that e-mail is a supplement to, not a substitute for, personal interaction.
- We won't spam.
- We will treat people electronically the same way we would in person.
- Instead of copying long quotes from others, we will briefly summarize them and add attachments, if necessary.

Figure 18.1   E-mail Protocol Examples

unwanted. This is defined not by the sender but by the receiver. For example, too many of us think it is OK to send out jokes and cute stories to the team *if we* send them, but it's *not* OK when *somebody else sends them to us.* Too many of the FYI type of e-mails may actually fall into this category. Although it is often like walking a tightrope, we need to send enough information to help other team members do their jobs, without sending so much that we unintentionally prevent them from doing their jobs. How do we know how much is too much? Ask. Unless we know they really need something they say they don't use, can the digital lunch meat.

Tip Number 10. Use e-mail filters to sort incoming mail. Filters allow you to eliminate considerable amounts of incoming spam simply by choosing key words and prohibiting e-mail with those key words in the subject line, text, and/or address line. Some distance managers told us that they excluded sentences like "take credit cards," "free vacation," or "XXX" and other statements frequently found in pornographic spam. One told us that multiple exclamation points in the subject line was a clear indicator of spam (and clumsy marketing). Others noted that series of numbers in the e-mail address was a giveaway. Most e-mail programs have a way of blocking messages from anyone once you tag them with a "send to trash" instruction. Check out your e-mail program to see how these features could work for you.

Tip Number 11. To avoid incoming spam, use a different screen name when you sign onto public message boards or use chat rooms. Lots of spammers get their addresses from these public arenas. If you use a different screen name than your e-mail screen name, it makes it more difficult to send you their unrequested stuff.

Tip Number 12. To avoid possible spamming by others, send out blind addresses when you e-mail a group. Blinding the addresses doesn't print out everyone on the "to" list and disallows some people on the list from getting the e-mail addresses of other recipients. The obvious exception to this rule is when the people listed on the e-mail have a business need to collaborate and contact each other. In this case you may be providing a service by sharing e-mail addresses that the collaborators have not yet given each other.

General Tips for Managing E-mail

Tip Number 13. Know how your recipients' systems are set up and send e-mail accordingly. Not everyone is set up for "rich text," for example, and your colorful note may just look like alien computer code to the recipient. Some ISPs have limitations on attachments. Are you sending something written in a program that your recipients may not have and will therefore be unable to open? Some programs have features that are only available to other people with the same program. At the time of this writing, for example, AOL users can see some of the fancy messages others send who are also AOL-supported, but advanced ones sent from Eudora are unreadable.

Tip Number 14. Keep your in-box lean. Use folders to organize your e-mail and keep the in-box small enough that you can scan it quickly for important messages. Some programs will sort mail automatically if you instruct them. For example, you could automatically put everything from your boss or key customers into an "urgent" file and put e-mail from family members and church or school associates into a "personal" file.

Tip Number 15. Manage your address book. Don't type addresses in unless you need to. Most programs allow automatic address book entry of anyone who sends you an e-mail, or anyone who you compose an e-mail to. If you keep it up to date and use it properly, the address book can save you a lot of time.

Tips for Dealing with Sensitive Issues

Tip Number 16. Never write something that is private or confidential on e-mail. Microsoft learned this the hard way in court. Messages that its employees thought were confidential, and in some cases, destroyed, came back to haunt them. Just because a message has been deleted doesn't mean it can't be exhumed from a hidden cache by a cyber sleuth.

Today, many distance managers are working across organization lines, sometimes dealing with sensitive information from other companies partnering on a project. This calls for extra effort to ensure that confidentiality is never breached and that corporate-sensitive information is treated with the utmost respect. This type of information should *never* go into e-mail.

Tip Number 17. Educate the team on appropriate and inappropriate use of e-mail. Companies are beginning to understand and experience firsthand the legal ramifications of this technology. Consider, for example, the *Fortune* 500 company that was ordered to pay $2.2 million to four plaintiffs in a sexual harassment suit based in part on an e-mail message that circulated about "why beer is better than women."[1] Or the unfortunate circumstance at the Norfolk, Virginia, office of *The New York Times,* where 23 employees were fired for sending what the company said was inappropriate e-mail.[2]

Because of increasing liability, many companies are creating ways to more tightly control and monitor e-mail. If your organization has an e-mail policy, make sure that everyone knows what it is, and that they understand what is acceptable according to corporate guidelines.

Tip Number 18. Don't open questionable e-mail. If you don't know the sender and/or the description line doesn't make sense to you, don't open it. It may just be spam, but it might also be an e-mail virus. The worst thing that can happen if you use this tip is that someone will be upset that you didn't answer their e-mail. Tell them why and encourage them to send any future e-mails to you in a way that will enable you to respond. Better safe than sorry.

Tip Number 19. Be careful of putting emotional content into e-mail. Although emoticons like the smiley face for humor ☺ or the frowning face for sad ☹ can help to more clearly express unclear emotions in e-mail, this can be very tricky business ("Is he serious or is he just making a joke?"). Be especially cautious about putting humor into an e-mail in teams that cross cultural distance. What is funny to one person may easily be offensive to another. Sarcasm, in particular, can be very problematic. Although you will frequently see shorthand for these types of statements (the widely used IMHO, for example, stands for "in my humble opinion"), you are better off steering clear of them and just using clear business language to avoid any misunderstanding.

One distance leader has suggested that if you are feeling emotional when you write an e-mail, send it to yourself before you send it to the other person. Don't read it until the next day. If you read it later and it still seems OK, then send it. But if you wonder, "What was I thinking when I wrote that!" start over and be glad that you didn't act impulsively.

Tip Number 20. Never use e-mail to address performance or interpersonal issues. We've all heard horror stories of managers enamored with technology who send a team member's performance appraisal via e-mail, or even worse, carry out a corrective action process electronically. When performance problems arise in virtual teams, it is incumbent on the distance manager to work those issues face-to-face. In crisis situations where there isn't time to travel to the site, hold a teleconference or videoconference.

Similarly, when helping team members work interpersonal issues with each other, get involved via phone or video. Resolving interpersonal issues typically requires some concentrated effort and significant conversation to assure that all parties have been heard and understood.

Summary

In this chapter we have reviewed a number of tips to help distance leaders manage one of the most useful (and problematic) technologies of the information age. We have shared specific tips for dealing with sensitive issues, such as legal, emotional, and confidentiality concerns. We also reviewed a few tips for general e-mail management and spam avoidance. One of the biggest challenges to the distance leader, however, is how to minimize e-mail glut. Some things that can help are to have a no-scrolling rule, avoid group replies, keep group lists up to date, quote only what is necessary, don't let e-mails build up, use the description line well, use automatic replies, and, of course, establish protocols for e-mail use with the team.

References

1. Jessica L. Lloyd-Rogers, "No Offense," *The Business Journal,* December 10, 1999. p. 24.
2. Kathleen Ohlson, "E-Mail Leads to Dismissals: *New York Times* Fires 23 Employees," *Computerworld,* December 6, 1999, p. 24.

Using Web Tools: Effective Shared Workplaces and Files

Protocols, not management, will govern interaction in the organizations of the future.[1]

Raymond E. Miles, Professor Emeritus
University of California at Berkeley

W HEN THE AUTHORS began writing this book together, we divided up the chapters and research assignments and began to work. Although we were frequently writing in airplanes or in different cities, it was important that we coordinate our work somehow and provide a way that each of us could see what the other was doing. We also agreed that each would edit the work of the other to provide a consistent voice and eliminate redundancies. The good news is that the technology exists to allow us to do this rather easily. The bad news is that there is a certain risk associated with shared files.

We decided to keep a draft of the work in progress on a central server on our company intranet that either one could access and modify. We each kept copies of our work on our individual portable computers as well. We agreed on what to name the files so that we wouldn't have multiple copies of a single chapter floating out there on the server. We designated a particular location for the files to avoid some chapters being saved (and lost) in different places. But we had both experienced problems using these types of shared files before, which made us nervous.

We wanted to avoid similar problems on this book. We became studious about checking dates before replacing files on the server, to ensure that we weren't accidentally overwriting newer files with older ones. Near the end of the project, especially, we established a number of protocols for working in the shared files, which we adhered to strictly. For example, in our daily meetings (usually held over the telephone in the evening while we were both in different cities) we separated our assignments so that we were never both working in the same file on the same day. We coordinated regularly who would update the server when and with what, to ensure that work was not lost. Although all of this coordination took time away from writing, it was necessary to avoid problems.

But it still wasn't enough. Although we aren't sure how it happened, as we neared the deadline, a problem occurred. One of the authors began a major revision of all the chapters while the other author was out of town. She worked directly from the server, spending about a week making the format and style consistent in all of the chapters and correcting spelling errors that couldn't be caught with the spell checker. Numerous hours were spent verifying quotes, adding and deleting stories and information, rewording long sections to make them clearer, and developing tables and graphics to support the chapters.

Confident that her editing pass was finally completed, she informed the other author that he could take his turn at making an editorial pass through the book as well as adding new chapters that he had been working on. He downloaded the book file from the server onto his portable computer and proceeded to work for several days, while she agreed not to make any additional changes.

The author who downloaded the revised file was later horrified to discover that the copy he had been working on did not include the first author's corrections. Had he accidentally overwritten the newer version he downloaded with the older one on his portable? Was there an older version on the server that he downloaded by mistake? Did he unintentionally allow the computer to revert to a previously saved file?

Now they had two copies of the first half of the book. His copy on his portable had his corrections, and her copy on the server had her corrections. Not only had they wasted time in repetitious activity (he had recorrected some of the mistakes she had already discovered), but they had to take several days to compare the chapters side by side to ensure that the improvements from both versions were incorporated into the final copy. At least a week's worth of work was lost just at the time when the deadline was looming.

As has been illustrated in this personal example, shared workspaces can be both a blessing and a curse. They enable distance work in a way that was simply impossible just a few years ago. But like most of the technologies we have reviewed in the book so far, if they are used improperly they can do more harm than good. We have heard stories from distance leaders about lost productivity and effectiveness. It's bad enough to lose a week's worth of work on a book. But what if you lose irreplaceable custom software, new products, or business plans? In this chapter we'll review some tips for lessening the risks of these problems and increasing the effectiveness of shared workplaces and files. First, however, let's briefly review some tools that make shared workspaces more effective.

Teamware

Teamware, also called *collaborative software systems* or *group support systems* (GSS), helps to coordinate team interaction and minimizes many problems like those mentioned in the case study that opens this chapter. Multiple author programs, for example, allow several different people to offer alternative versions of a written paragraph in a business plan or customer proposal without overwriting the original. By showing the proposed revision in a distinctive form (e.g., highlighted, italicized, bolded, underlined, different color), team members can consider alternatives with less risk of important content loss. Most popular word processing programs now carry similar features as well, although they may not be as easy to use as programs designed specifically for groups.

There are GSS programs that facilitate everything from sharing calendars and phone books to synchronous collaboration on project management activities, brainstorming, decision making and problem solving, customer relationships management, computer-aided design

(CAD) systems, financial management, complicated database management, and a host of other applications.

Tips for Effective Shared Workspace

Tip Number 1. Use teamware. If good (both effective *and* user-friendly) software exists for your most common collaborative applications, you are usually money ahead to invest in it.

Tip Number 2. Train people how to work together in shared applications. As our experience shows, buying software doesn't by itself solve anything. You also need to train people on how to use the software, hardware, network, and other technical tools necessary to work together. Also remember to train people on the company policies, ethics, and etiquette that affect this type of work.

Tip Number 3. Do regular backups. The risk of data loss or corruption increases exponentially with multiple users working on the same files. Choose a regular backup system that works for you. A popular way to do this is by using a software program that automatically backs up the server and individual hard disks on a regular basis. Some people prefer manually saving to tapes, dedicated hard drives used just for backup, on-line storage, or other backup methods.

Tip Number 4. Establish protocols. What are your team's rules for working together this way? One organization, for example, equates the most current version of a file to a football and assigns the responsibility of managing it by asking "who's got the football today?" in the daily team meeting. Protocols address other issues as well. Is it OK to log onto a brainstorming session anonymously or not? Who will record the minutes from a decision-making session? How will next steps be assigned? How will the decisions about who facilitates a session get made? Will you rotate these kinds of assignments? What is the manager's role in these activities? What will we name files? Where will they be located? Who can change things on shared files? What process will we use to authorize changes? Answering these kinds of questions will help the team work much more productively together.

Tip Number 5. Don't use confusing file names. We once had an employee who named the most current files "latest." When she updated a version of our leadership training program, for example, she would name it "Leadership Skills-latest." This soon became very confusing as numerous files were called latest. Although it was possible to check file creation dates, this was burdensome and got in the way when we were doing searches based on file names. Eventually, as we improved the "latest" files, we decided to add the month and year to the file name in order to avoid the problem of having multiple versions of a file with the same name. This is not the only scenario where file names can be confusing. What makes sense to one team member may confuse another. Whenever multiple people are sharing files, they should all have some say in how they are named and organized.

Tip Number 6. If you are sharing desktop space, be clear about what goes where and what belongs to whom. Shared desktop space can be problematic, as we have discussed in earlier chapters. If you have to do it, be clear about what is personal property and what is shared property. Allow enough customization of the personal space to enable the team member to really feel like he or she "owns" that part of cyber real estate. Have protocols for the common space. These suggestions apply to servers as well. Many organizations find it useful to have team and/or individual folders on the server desktop as a way of facilitating data transfer and to provide a certain degree of personalization within the public space. Do what makes sense in your operation.

Summary

Web tools such as teamware and other shared workspace software and networks provide a wonderful way to collaborate on product development, report writing, customer relations management, project management, and other problem-solving and decision-making activities. But these empowering technologies can also backfire if they aren't used properly. Taking the time to choose the right tools, deciding how to use them, and monitoring their effectiveness over time are necessary to avoid problems and improve productivity.

Reference

1. From a presentation made at the Brigham Young University Organizational Behavior Conference, Provo, Utah, March 31, 2000.

Web Conferencing: Working with Whiteboards and Web Meetings

We have board members in France, Germany, and California and we have every third or fourth meeting face-to-face. But the in-between meetings use our own [Web conferencing] service. We think it's easier and more effective than just teleconference or videoconferences because it's such a clean process.

Bill Barhydt, President and CEO
WebSentric

W EBSENTRIC IS A company that helps other companies hold meetings over the Internet. It started in 1998 with only four people near

Munich, Germany. Financed with German venture capital, WebSentric grew rapidly to 60-plus people spread over three countries. The company currently has offices in San Mateo, Munich, New York, London, and Portland, and plans to open others soon in Chicago and Paris. A Tokyo office is likely to open soon.

"You do have to travel a lot," WebSentric CEO Bill Barhydt confirms, when asked how he spends his time managing his rapidly expanding operation. What are the biggest challenges? "Finding a way to deal with the time differences," he says. He also offers some practical advice. "Make sure your cell phone number works in all the countries you visit," he says, "and make your calendar electronically available to everybody who needs to see it." Any employee in his company can now access the calendars, new-product updates, company e-mail, and newsgroups portions of the company intranet.

To facilitate business and simplify e-mail communications, WebSentric decided early on to become its own Internet service provider (ISP) rather than contracting with someone else. Its managers quickly discovered how important these types of communication systems were to them. "We found out that we needed to have a good IT person in each location, even when we outsource it," says Barhydt. This allows people to maintain the information systems that even small distance organizations come to rely upon.

The WebSentric organization has become an ideal test case for its own services. By creating a technology that allows people to work from any platform and to cross multiple firewalls, WebSentric has developed a turnkey method for real-time meetings between people scattered across geography.

Bill Barhydt's staff meetings are conducted this way. "The staff meetings are held every week at 8:00 A.M. U.S. Pacific Standard Time regardless of where I am at the time," he says. The seven staff members are divided between the United States and Germany, with people representing sales, marketing, engineering, finance, and business development functions. "At least once every two months we need a face-to-face meeting," says Barhydt. "Don't assume you can completely replace face-to-face meetings. You can't. But in between we share weekly updates with each other over the Internet."

Each staff member normally puts together about a 15-minute Power Point™ presentation to review highlights from the week's activities. A coordinator is selected for each meeting to help plan and facilitate it. Special emphasis is placed on sales collateral—the sales data sheets, sales presentations, and new-features discussions necessary to get their fledgling operation into full flight. By using their own service and other aids they have learned to minimize the problems associated with managing across time, space, and culture.

One of the key challenges in distance management is getting team members to meet together in real time. Fortunately, a number of technologies facilitate this, as illustrated by the WebSentric case. Some of these technologies are beginning to approximate the effectiveness of face-to-face meetings, even if they can't completely replace them. In this chapter we will review a number of methods for meeting in cyberspace, and suggest some tips for how to make several different types of meetings and training sessions more effective.

Effective Web Meetings

Some of the most powerful Internet applications for distance work are Web conferencing aids. Like other distance technologies that we have already described, however, Web meetings require more effective planning and facilitation than their face-to-face counterparts. There should be a clear set of objectives and an agenda for each meeting. This helps the facilitator keep the meeting on track by asking questions like, "Are we focusing on the right things to accomplish our meeting's purpose?" or, "We're only one-third of the way through our agenda even though our time is two-thirds over. Do we need to adjust our agenda?"

See Chapter 16, "The Distance Manager's Guide to Efficient Teleconferences," for tips on distance meeting facilitation that apply as much to Web meetings as they do to teleconferences. Remember two things in particular: (1) keep the length of the meetings short (we recommend no longer than two hours), and (2) find ways to create active involvement in the meetings. It's hard enough to pay attention in a Web meeting when you have a responsibility as a leader, scribe, or gatekeeper. But it is almost humanly impossible to be fully attentive in a Web meeting where you spend most of your time quietly listening to long presentations from others while you gaze at the computer. Create excuses for interaction (e.g., polling, surveys, discussion periods, making something together). If you just want people to look at something and respond to it, you probably don't even need a Web meeting—just send everybody an e-mail with a document or video attachment.

Here are a few other tips for managing these meetings:

Tip Number 1. Try to engage as many of the participants' senses as you can in Web meetings. Having everyone watch a presentation together is good, but doing it while they type e-mail-like comments to each other is better. Still better is adding audio teleconferencing for real-time discussions. Incorporating video is another help (if you use it for something more than allowing people to watch a talking head like some of those horrible general education college courses). In response to team members' questions, use it to demonstrate how you might show a customer or investor your product. Or point a camera at someone who is having a technical problem with some software so people can help troubleshoot it in real time. If it's a need you can foresee, prepare short video clips before the meeting and incorporate them into the presentation. This is especially effective for things like product demonstrations or case vignettes (when you are doing training). See Chapter 17, "Videoconferencing: Technology and Table Manners" to review other tips on using video.

Tip Number 2. Record Web meetings for absent members. Distance teams often have difficulty finding a time when all team members can meet. Get a technology that allows you to record a Web meeting so that it can be played back later for members who were unable to make the original meeting. It's not as good as being there, and shouldn't be a regular substitution for personal involvement, but it's a lot better than nothing. It may also be helpful for people whose first language is not the language the meeting was held in. They can later review the Web conference at their own speed to increase their comprehension of the proceedings.

Tip Number 3. Manage the logistics. Make sure that the participants have sufficient notice regarding when the meeting will be, how long it will last, and what assignments they may have to complete prior to and after the meeting. Sometimes, meeting failure can be avoided just by being sufficiently prepared. For example, can everybody actually connect up to the meeting? Sometimes that new free software a team member just downloaded on their computer may cause a conflict that disables certain Web meeting functions. Is anyone's browser cache so full that it inhibits them from downloading the presentation? It's better to know about these kinds of problems prior to a meeting than to have to waste everybody else's time while the team member in Denver is absent and unaccounted for.

Tip Number 4. Do a quick technology check at the beginning of each conference. Don't take a lot of time doing this, but do a quick test of the different technologies you'll be using during the meeting before you begin. If you'll be using a polling feature during the meeting, for example, ask each site to test this by asking a sample question to get their responses. This prevents disappointing mistakes later on when you find out that Chicago's polling data wasn't included in the meeting because it didn't work properly or because they forgot how to do it. Make sure that everybody can hear everybody else. Have them adjust their volumes or distances from the microphones appropriately. Don't assume that people will tell you if things aren't working properly—ask and find out.

Using Whiteboards

Whiteboards can be another useful Web tool to facilitate team interaction. There are at least a couple of different types of whiteboards. The large whiteboards that are wall-sized and connected to the Internet can send a picture of whatever is drawn on them to whoever is at the meeting. Personal whiteboards or drawing tablets can also be connected as a computer peripheral. You can also create virtual whiteboards. Using shared graphics files allows multiple meeting members to modify a drawing that everyone can see on their computer screens at the same time.

Using any of these whiteboards can add a different dimension to your meeting. You can draw simple blueprints, sketch a diagram of where everybody is supposed to meet in the hotel next week, or draw out the schedule to see if everyone understands when their part of the project is due. A designated facilitator can display handwritten meeting notes that aren't limited to words. We have observed meetings at Hewlett-Packard, for example, where the facilitators included diagrams, models, charts, schedules, and even cartoons in the meeting notes. Interactive whiteboard capability opens the door to still more options. Team members can review and then revise the sketch of the new product, or pencil in suggestions or watch-outs on the critical path schedule.

Tips for Using Whiteboards

Tip Number 5. Have a protocol for how to change shared graphics. If you have interactive whiteboard capability, is it OK for anyone to erase and revise a portion of a graphic, or do you need to talk about it first? Do you want everyone to have "the power of the pen," or will you take turns being the person who revises? Will you trade scribe responsibilities or will you designate a notetaker for the entire meeting?

Tip Number 6. Use whiteboards like a chart pad. One of the advantages of a face-to-face meeting that is well-facilitated is that you can use a chart pad to record ideas, take notes, make assignments, and so forth. The value of doing this publicly is that it allows everyone to see what is written down so they can agree or disagree with it.

We can't tell you the number of times we have seen people walk out of the same meeting with very different interpretations of what transpired. This is exacerbated over time, space, and culture. Instead of allowing everyone to have their own interpretation of a group decision, for example, have the scribe write it down on the whiteboard. Ask, "Is this what we agreed to?" and get a response from everyone. During group activities like brainstorming this public display of people's ideas as they are created is essential to making the process work. It allows people to come up with other ideas that are triggered by something they see written down. It is also a good idea to end each meeting with a list of the assignments that were made during the meeting. This provides clarification and more effective accountability. Although a whiteboard is not the only way to do this, it works well.

Summary

Web meetings are a useful tool for distance work. When used properly they can facilitate knowledge transfer and coordinate interaction almost as well as a face-to-face meeting. But they take some preparation and facilitation to be effective. Whiteboards can add a nice dimension to these meetings by allowing people to display and revise graphics and notes they create in real time. Web meetings with audio and video can enable richer communication. And the Web, the overarching support technology that allows these types of meetings, can be a tremendous blessing (or curse, if mismanaged) to the distance leader.

4

The Distance Manager in Action

The Distance Sales Manager at Xerox

Even though we have good technology for working over distances, we've found that there is a certain amount of synergy that you can only get from being face-to-face.

Eric Ecklund, National Account Manager,
Public Sector, Xerox

Eric Ecklund is currently a national account manager (NAM) for Xerox's public sector sales operations, based in Portland, Oregon. His personal territory covers Oregon and Idaho and his responsibilities include managing large public accounts such as city, county, and state governments, school districts, and universities throughout the two states. He must coordinate carefully with salespeople who work with public account customers as well as with other national account managers located in Washington, Idaho, Utah, New Mexico, Colorado, Arizona, Missouri, and California.

This is a very fluid organization. "We have reorganized frequently the last few years," he notes, "and I could have a different assignment by the time the book gets published, but I've been in some type of sales position for all of my career at Xerox."

His NAM team has been very successful. They were the number one team of their type in the company for three years in a row. Ecklund's current assignment has been growing at 10 to 15 percent annually. They currently have over $24 million a year in billed revenue across all Xerox delivery channels in his area alone.

In this chapter we will review both Ecklund's work as a NAM—where he must influence and coordinate a number of salespeople who do not report to him directly—and as a national account team member that works with other NAMs across the United States to develop and coordinate national accounts.

The Challenges of Sales Leadership from a Distance

Ecklund has the unique position of being both a team leader and a team member in Xerox sales. This gives him a very helpful perspective for those attempting to learn more about distance sales leadership. The salespeople he leads report not to him but to their own public sector line leadership. In more rural locations, sales are also made by Xerox agents whose time is spent in public sector sales (Ecklund's area of responsibility) and commercial sales as well. The percentage of time varies from agent to agent, but most spend only a relatively small amount of their time in public sales. A commensurately small amount of their commissions come from these activities. So Ecklund has a significant challenge. With no direct "position power" (he isn't their boss), and with relatively little leverage on a fair percentage of the commissions of the sales force he supports as a national account manager, how can he motivate and coordinate those within his area of responsibility?

In his assignment on the national account team Ecklund encounters additional difficulties. Although he is a team member rather than a team leader in this case, he must find a way (with the leadership support of his boss) to coordinate with others he seldom sees.

"It's a challenge," he reports, "but there are some things that help." Technology is one of the most important of these things.

Get Hooked Up

Four to five years ago, Xerox made a big push to provide computer technology to sales so they could link up effectively with customers, the rest of the company, and each other. Everyone got a laptop computer, e-mail, a voice mailbox for their cell phone, and a pager. Ecklund uses his den at home for a virtual office and has a copy and fax machine there. Xerox pays for a second phone line in the sales reps' homes to provide dedicated business access for customer calls and data transmission.

More recently, a company Web site to facilitate document storage and interaction has also been established. It has a powerful search engine to sort through the suggestions and best practices listed on the site. Practices are posted to provide recognition for employees and to enable better transfer of ideas. There is free conference room capability for setting up a Web conference and an on-line chat room. The sales reps also have access to a videoconference center for video meetings. Teleconferences are common. They are useful for salespeople, who often have multiple requirements on their time.

Salespeople connect from their homes to a server located in their brick-and-mortar office. They retain an office for occasional interaction, but spend the bulk of their time working at home or from customer sites. For example, they can now create pricing contracts remotely on the server instead of going to the office. What used to take hours is almost instantaneous (travel time to the office is reduced, and basic electronic templates and examples mean the contracts don't have to be created from scratch). And most important, now everyone has access to everyone else's contracts. This facilitates open information sharing and helps to generate ideas. ("Hey, I noticed that you did this for your customer—I think that would work for mine, too.") The software used to facilitate this storage and retrieval process is called Docushare®, and it is so successful that Xerox now markets it to its clients.

It's not just the fact that they are virtual that makes these types of technologies useful. Much of it is driven by customers who expect the salespeople to respond to e-mail and interact with them over the Web. "They want us to have a Web site where they can do virtual demo of our equipment," he says. "We need the PCs and server connections to get current price sheets and respond to requests for proposals. If we lost our computers we'd be sunk." As evidence of their dependence on these technologies, Ecklund points to the problem the sales reps sometimes have connecting to the server. "We have 15 lines coming into 4 servers. If you don't connect up by 7:30 in the morning, you might not get access." He notes that part of the problem is caused by modem speed at the remote home offices that don't have broadband connections. "Download time can be too long. Watch this pretty carefully," he cautions. "It's pretty bad to be at a customer site trying to download a current price list, when you either can't get on a server, or it takes too long to do it."

Another technology Ecklund finds useful is the distance training activities sponsored by Xerox. The salespeople have a satellite hookup to world-class training programs and also use Web training. "It's great," he says. "We used to have to travel and be in classes for about two weeks a year to get the training we now get on-line." Surveys, tests, and self-study programs are available. They also have fairly regular town-hall-type meetings with the top brass. "There is a 1-800 number you call to ask questions. It's good. You feel more connected and informed."

Virtual Offices Don't Always Work

Ecklund cautions that in some cases the virtual office setup can go too far. For example, in a test case in a sales office a few years ago, all of the salespeople were taken out of the office to work exclusively from their cars and homes. The local sales managers met once a week to coordinate things, and there were monthly sales meetings for the local sales force. Even though the real estate savings for eliminating the office was significant, the sales organization found that the complete abandonment of some sort of common office set up was detrimental.

They ended up putting some minimum office space back in, with meeting places and dedicated cubicles for some of the reps that need it the most. They use the hoteling concept introduced earlier in the book for the rest of the office area. In this part of the office, small networked office space is available to sales reps on a first-come, first-served basis.

The informal interaction that occurs when people come in to use an office space was an important justification for reestablishing it. Confirms Steven Ramirez, a vice president and quality officer for the U.S. customer operations of Xerox, "We had cost savings for the buildings, but sales dropped. Why? Because there wasn't enough interaction. People weren't telling war stories; we needed more knowledge transfer. We had to add some offices back in to provide some group areas for information sharing."[1] Ramirez also suggests that it isn't general knowledge sharing that is important—it's practice sharing. It's not just what you know, it's what you do. "Implemented practices are what contribute to business success," he says. When interacting face-to-face, salespeople share tips and techniques and help to motivate each other in ways that are difficult to do electronically.

Challenges with Recognition

One of the challenges that Ecklund has experienced in the current virtual organization is how to handle recognition. Although Xerox can do a number of things to deal with individual commissions and the financial portions of the reward and recognition system, Ecklund is convinced that salespeople thrive on more public forms of praise and recognition. In the more traditional operation that preceded the current setup, Ecklund and others had fairly frequent public forums in which they could stand and recognize accomplishments by saying something like, "This month Tony is 400 percent of plan!" This has become increasingly difficult now that groupwide face-to-face interaction is far less frequent.

Ecklund still meets with the sales reps several times during the year. Although these meetings are very helpful—essential, in fact, to keep the public accounts coordinated—sales goals are monitored on a more frequent (monthly) basis. Thus it is difficult to maintain a consistent momentum when positive or negative events like a big sale, a new product or promotion, or a big cancellation occur during a month when there is no meeting.

Since there are now fewer of these meetings, each of them has become more important. "In some ways being in sales is like being in boot camp," explains Ecklund. "You work better when you share a common bond with each other." This bond is difficult to create at a distance.

Sales reps, like soldiers, need a lot of joint encouragement and motivation because their work can be tedious, difficult, and discouraging. "You have to do a lot of 'rah-rah,' " Ecklund says, referring to the fun, high-energy activities needed to recharge and reenergize the sales force.

Team Building in Distance Sales Organizations

Ecklund reinforces the importance of regular team building activities for sales organizations. For the NAM team, for example, he believes their team-building sessions—held in conjunction with what used to be quarterly and what have recently been changed to semiannual retreats—have been very useful. "We usually have meetings in the mornings and then we try to have some sort of a fun activity like golfing in the afternoon. This helps us to rebuild our relationships that we depend on in between our retreats." He is convinced that distance sales work requires these sorts of activities as a lubricant to make things go more smoothly during the rest of the year.

These team building sessions help the regular teleconferences with Ecklund's manager and NAM team members to be more effective as well. They schedule teleconferences as required to supplement their regularly scheduled monthly telephone meeting that normally lasts about two hours. Trust and confidence in others increases as a result of the team building, and there is less need for nonproductive "cover-your-butt" activities or the political posturing that is more common when working with virtual strangers at a distance. They can just get down to business.

Avoiding Information Overload

Another thing that Eric Ecklund appreciates about his team leader is the way he shields the team from information overload. "The new technologies are a mixed blessing," he says. "Although they make it a lot easier to coordinate and communicate with each other, they also make it easier to get inundated with information. I could easily spend most every day just reading and responding to e-mails if my manager wasn't screening and responding to a lot of those for us." He estimates that his boss screens out about 50 percent of the information he receives, to get to the portion that the NAMs really benefit from knowing. This reduces the administrative workload of the salespeople and NAMs alike. Although Ecklund has administrative support based in California and Florida, he must still do more of this work than he used to do because the e-mails and information come directly to him and not to an office assistant. Every unnecessary e-mail he has to read and respond to is time lost working with customers or sales reps.

Summary

While the distance sales manager faces a number of specific challenges associated with coordinating and motivating sales reps, the experiences of managers like Eric Ecklund at Xerox illustrate some helpful practices to address these challenges. Their experience clearly demonstrates, for example, the importance of having the electronic equipment necessary for communicating on a regular basis and the value of face-to-face meetings for building teams and enthusiasm. Finally, it cautions us about taking virtual teaming too far or becoming subject to information overload.

Reference

1. Steven Ramirez, Presentation at the University of North Texas Center for the Study of Work Teams conference, 1998.

The Distance Project Manager at International Paper

As leader of the lead team, Jim [Hoffmann] truly is in the role of enabling and assisting, not prescribing or directing. He learns what people want to do and then helps them grow and develop.

Jim Garvin, Senior Consultant
International Paper Partnership Project

EFFECTIVE DISTANCE MANAGERS know how to manage projects. On the surface this can appear to be fairly straightforward. Project team members need an understanding of the project expectations (including the so-called "big three"—cost, scope, and schedule), a good plan for achieving them (with objectives and mileposts), clearly defined responsibilities (who will do what by when), and lots and lots of communication to deal with the inevitable setbacks, coordination problems, and revisions. But in organizations—especially in virtual organizations—things are often not as easy as they appear. How do you manage multiple projects at one time without too much confusion, redundancy, or dilution of effort? How do team members get project updates when they aren't co-located? How do learnings from one project get transferred to another one so that each new team can benefit from earlier experiences?

In this chapter we will review an extraordinary story of how a distance project leader does this work. We will learn how he coordinates the activities of multiple projects with a team spread all over the United States.

The Project Team

Jim Hoffmann, a former middle school principal, is the team leader of a very unique project—or more accurately, he is the team leader of a series of projects spread across the country. With the support of his employer, International Paper, he and a sterling cadre of 10 independent consultants are working to improve middle school education in selected U.S. cities where the company has mills. Originally created by Champion International Corporation, International Paper decided to continue the project when they purchased Champion in 2000. Why would an industrial giant do this? Partly because the Partnership project provides some good public relations, but mostly because I.P. feels the endeavor is a good way to give something back to the communities in which their employees live. It is a superb example of corporate magnanimity.

Hoffmann's team is currently working on major change projects in 58 schools in 10 states, with plans to expand into additional schools and geographic locations. Team members include many of the leading U.S. authorities on middle school education, all of whom have advanced degrees. Most work part-time on the team and part-time on their own consulting projects. Some work as professors at universities.

Hoffmann is located in Stamford, Connecticut, and other members of the lead team are spread across multiple states and time zones. He faces the challenge of coordinating the project activities of a group of world-class experts (a process akin to herding cats), as well as managing a virtual team where many of its members have their primary allegiance elsewhere (e.g., the professors are on tenure tracks at the respective universities where they are employed).

The Partnership Team

The 10 consultants are part of what is called the *lead team* (see Figure 22.1). The lead team coordinates the activities of all of the projects. Hoffmann is the team leader. The consultants are also members of two other teams. Champion Leadership teams (CLTs) reside at the school level. They are composed of the principal, teachers, and one lead team member. The CLTs' primary responsibilities are assessing school needs and planning and monitoring staff development. A site team is comprised of two to five lead team members. The site teams are responsible for coordination and implementation of site-based partnership activities. All three teams—the lead team, the CLT, and the site team—must work closely together to implement the school improvements.

TEAM OPERATIONAL CHART

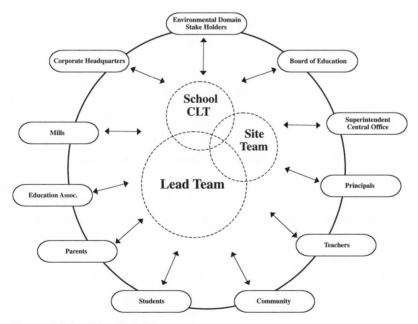

Figure 22.1   The CLT Diagram

Results

It is already clear that the Partnership project is a success. Hoffmann's team is the recipient of numerous prestigious awards and very positive public relations for what one vice president calls "doing God's work." Even more important, in the schools where they have completed their projects successfully, parental support has doubled, student behavior has improved, student scores are higher, and teachers are enthusiastic about opportunities to network with colleagues from other schools, learn new ways to teach, and stay current on the latest innovations in teaching.

What has helped this project team be so successful? Contributing factors include strong, consistent leadership, ongoing team member development, formal and informal communication methodologies, and well-orchestrated team start-up activities—including the creation of core values, operating guidelines, and clearly defined boundaries and team member roles and responsibilities. Says Neila Connors, a member of the lead team, "As a member of an extraordinary virtual team, it is evident that the broad dynamics for the team's success include commitment, communication, support, the ability to listen and learn, and a continued appraisal of the mission statement. The specifics incorporate the personalities and passion of the individual team members combined with the ability to have fun and benefit from the adventure."

The Leadership Factor

The consultants suggest several leadership practices that help to make Hoffmann so effective in managing from a distance. Their recommendations for other project leaders includes these five practices:

1. Be accessible. Says Jerry Lynch, lead team member and director of the Quinnesec site team, "What makes this team so good is that leadership is accessible. We never go more than 12 hours without being able to contact Jim [Hoffmann] or each other." Echoes James Gautier, also a lead team member, "Jim [Hoffmann] calls regularly to ask how things are going. He always asks, 'What can we [International Paper] do to help you?' or, 'What do you need to be effective?' Jim doesn't call only when there is bad news."

2. Eliminate blaming. It is easy to jump to conclusions about the motives or intent of others, especially when you don't have the advantage of casual "hallway" interaction which might serve as an opportunity to clear up potential misunderstandings. But according to the consultants, Hoffmann doesn't do that. He assumes good intentions on the part of team members who aren't co-located, and then coaches to improve actions, outcomes, processes, or procedures in a supportive and collegial way.

3. Create a learning environment. Effective knowledge transfer is essential to virtual teams, but it is very difficult to facilitate from a distance. However, because of Hoffmann's leadership style, consultants report seeing little advantage in hoarding information—a situation that unfortunately may not be true in operations where blaming, high levels of peer competitiveness, or unchecked egos are allowed to continue.

4. Create personal development opportunities. As "head coach" of the Middle School Partnership, Hoffmann creates a variety of developmental activities such as reading and discussing state-of-the-art literature, inviting topic experts to address quarterly meetings, and visits to Partnership sites.

5. Manage work/life balance issues. Every lead team member has a remarkable commitment to the mission of the Middle School Partnership. This enthusiasm and dedication, if not properly channeled, could become all-consuming and take its toll on the individual or his or her family. Lead team member and consultant Howard Johnston explains, "The philosophy of the Middle School Partnership is to 'consider the whole child.' This means that we focus on all parts of life, not just the classroom. The dichotomy, however, is that because of our passion for this work, we sometimes immerse ourselves in the project to the detriment of our 'whole selves.' As project leader, Jim serves as a conscience to remind the lead team that their personal well-being is crucial to the ongoing health of the project."

Quarterly Face-to-Face Meetings

In addition to leadership effectiveness, a strong communication infrastructure (both formal and informal) is critical to the success of any virtual team. For example, the lead team members agree that quarterly face-to-face meetings are critical to maintaining the appropriate level of sharing and learning. During these meetings they conduct project reviews, upgrade the change template, learn from other experts brought in from the outside, engage in team building, and catch up with each other. The quarterly meetings have been an essential resource for managing the complexities of multiple simultaneous projects.

But quarterly meetings alone would be completely inadequate. Even though consultants spend the vast majority of their time with the schools, they are in almost daily communication with either Hoffmann or some other member of the lead team through e-mail or telephone calls. Their collaboration is too useful to be limited to four times a year.

Identifying Communication Preferences

Every member of the lead team acknowledges the vital role that communication protocols—agreements on how and how often they will communicate—have played in their ability to share information, stay informed, make decisions, and solve problems. At one lead team meeting each member discussed which method(s) of communication he or she prefers (e.g., e-mail, voice mail, telephone, written word). Once the other members understood each individual's preference they used that method to interact with that person as much as possible. They report that using these stated preferences improved the communication process.

Investing in Useful Technologies

Another key to the Middle School Partnership staff's success as a virtual team is access to appropriate technologies. Early in the process of getting the projects up and running, International Paper invested in some important communication-enhancing technologies. Each lead team member has an Internet-enabled notebook computer with a modem. They each have an e-mail address, and an intranet was developed to enable communication and project reviews between consultants in between quarterly meetings. Importantly, the Web site (middleschool .com) has an extranet feature that allows Partnership schools to learn more about other middle school projects and to access resources (announcements regarding upcoming conferences, training events, books, etc.) that may be useful to them.

Getting Off to a Good Start

Perhaps no other factor is as critical to a virtual team's long-term success as a good start-up. While co-located teams can regroup more easily if they encounter glitches in their operation, virtual teams may have great difficulty resolving problems and moving ahead if their start-up strategies are weak. During their start-up, the Middle School Partnership lead team accomplished five key objectives. They: (1) created a clear mission statement (see Figure 22.2), (2) defined boundary conditions, (3) articulated their core values, (4) established team operating guidelines, and (5) carefully defined team member roles and responsibilities. The team members believe that each of these activities was critical in helping them be more effective than they otherwise would have been. Let's discuss each of these five things in a little more detail:

1. *Mission statement.* An inspiring mission will help any team move ahead and will encourage its members to dedicate themselves to

---

MISSION (Team Charter)

What We Want to Do
Assist interested public school districts in International Paper communities in the redesigning of their middle level schools through staff development.

Why We Want to Do It
To improve student learning and enhance the quality of the students' lives.

How We'll Accomplish That
Utilizing the recommendations of the Carnegie report on adolescent development, *Turning Points: Preparing American Youth for the 21st Century.*

Figure 22.2   The Mission of the International Paper Middle School Partnership

the success of a project or cause. The middle school lead team is no exception. Team members are motivated and passionate about their cause. Howard Johnston puts it this way: "This is a wholesome project. How can you find anything wrong with helping kids and helping the teachers that help the kids? The human value of what we do is very dynamic." Consistency in mission also provides needed focus. Says John Van Hoose, lead team member and director of the Roanoke Rapids site team about the mission they developed, "We have had a mission statement since we started. It has helped enhance the kids' learning because we know what we do and what we don't do. For instance, when someone in the school wants to hire a psychologist or get 12 new computers, [we know that] we don't do that. We do staff development."

2. *Boundary conditions.* Clear boundary conditions also provide focus for the Partnership project. Says lead team member Judy Enright, "After the second meeting I knew what the boundaries were. But I don't feel constrained by them. We know what the parameters are and that keeps us from going off and pursuing our own agendas. It helps that this is modeled from the top down. Company vice president Bob Turner models this; Jim [Hoffmann] models this; and I feel that I can model this."

3. *Core values.* Articulating a set of core values (see Figure 22.3) served as a trust- and team building process for the lead team during the start-up. This document has subsequently provided an anchor for lead team members when consulting, making decisions, or problem solving in remote locations.

4. *Operating guidelines* (see Figure 22.4). The lead team's guidelines and core values go hand in hand. Like the core values document, the operating guidelines provide a sort of anchor—but they are more focused on the operational side of their work.

5. *Roles and responsibilities.* Once the mission was articulated, boundaries defined, and core values and operating guidelines established, the team was ready to discuss team member roles and responsibilities. Working from remote sites and meeting as a whole team only four times a year required that each team member be clear about his or her expected contribution to the proj-

Core Values

We believe:

- In a passionate commitment to the success and well-being of young adolescents and their public school communities.
- In focusing and refocusing on our clearly defined mission.
- In assisting and enabling the evolution of all Partnership schools through staff development in a patient, persistent, deliberative, and collaborative manner.
- In building relationships based on honest and sincere respect and support for Partnership teams and individuals.
- In creating opportunities to help others feel validated to grow.
- In the Partnership's ability to make a difference in the lives and performance of administrators, teachers, and students in public schools.

Figure 22.3   The Values of the International Paper Middle School Partnership

Middle School Partnership
Operational Guidelines
(Norms)

To fulfill the Partnership Mission, the Lead Team ascribes to these norms:

- We apply the "reasonable person" test to all that we do.
- We apply the appropriate company and Middle School Partnership norms in all of our work.
- We keep team members informed if what we do affects them or their work.
- We support strong relationships with time, money, and energy.
- We engage in continuous consultation with other team members to sustain trust and positive interdependence.
- We are tough on issues and ideas and easy on people.
- We always think win/win.
- We often move slowly in order to advance swiftly.

Figure 22.4   The Operating Guidelines

LEAD TEAM R-CHART

Decisions	Lead Team	Site Team	Regional Director	Site Manager	School Consultant	Partnership Manager	Senior Consultant	Team Leader	Tech Team	Tech Team Consultant	All Individuals	Executive Director	Vice President
Calendar	R												
School Expenditures					R								
Tech Team Expenditures									R				
Consultant Travel Expenses											R		
Personnel												R	A
Consultant Contracts												R	A
Partnership Budget	R											R	A
Operational Policies	R												
Summer Institute													
Regional Conferences	A	R		S									
Teacher Institute	R	R											
Site Assignments											C	R	
Site Team Budget		R										R	

214

*Only one "R" on each horizontal decision line.

R - Responsibility
The responsibility to initiate action, to ensure that the decision is carried out.

A - Approval
Approval required or the right to veto.
The particular items must be reviewed by the particular role occupant, and this person has the option of either vetoing or approving.

S - Support
Provide logistical support.

C - Consult
Get input from but not the decider.

I - Inform
Be informed, by inference, must not influence.

Figure 22.5   Lead Team R-Chart

215

ect's success. The lead team uses an "R Chart" (see Figure 22.5). This represents a discussion about who is responsible for something versus who must simply be informed about it. This is discussed and updated at quarterly meetings. Team members concur that clarity of roles keeps confusion, disappointment, conflict, and errors to a minimum.

The key to these start-up activities was that each lead team member participated in developing the five products. With the exception of the boundaries, they represent a collection of agreements made with each other, rather than an executive mandate.

Summary

By looking at an extraordinary project team dealing with multiple challenges, we can see some things that positively enable a distance project leader to be successful. Having a clear and compelling vision is important. Five leadership behaviors mentioned by lead team members that can also help virtual teams to be more effective include: accessibility, eliminating blame, fostering a learning environment, creating personal development opportunities, and managing work/life balance. In addition, good communication processes and an effective start-up, where they (1) created a clear mission statement, (2) defined boundary conditions, (3) articulated their core values, (4) established team operating guidelines, and (5) carefully defined team member roles and responsibilities, were critical to the effectiveness of these projects. Due to the work of this extraordinary band of consultants and the generosity first of Champion International Corporation, and then of International Paper, a lot of middle schools in the United States now are better places for teachers to work in and, most important, better places for kids to receive a high-quality education.

The Distance Product Development Manager at Hewlett-Packard

We use technology as a framework [for product development]. It is loosely structured to allow the use of numerous tools. The old monolithic approach is an accident waiting to happen. We need to empower people to integrate any tool they need.

Dion Eusepi, Process Technology Manager
Hewlett-Packard

HIGH-TECH GIANT HEWLETT-PACKARD has been challenged by CEO Carly Fiorina to regain the innovation and responsiveness that characterized the company when it was still operating out of a garage. Part of that challenge is a goal to reduce product development cycle times by a remarkable 50 percent in parts of the company. What makes this a Herculean effort is the fact that HP is already a recognized leader in rapidly getting its products to market. But in the high-tech industry, yesterday's performance is never good enough for today.

Many (perhaps most) of the development teams that design new products and services for Hewlett-Packard are virtual teams that cross time, space, and culture. Team members are selected for their expertise rather than to enable convenient working relationships. Consequently, it is not unusual to have team members represent various organizations and live in different states or countries. Membership might even include external vendors, key technology consultants, or a professor from Stanford University.

Travel time for everyone to fly to California or Idaho for team meetings is now sometimes a bottleneck in the critical-path schedule to meet the aggressive cycle time reduction requirements. The bulk of their work, often entailing the integration of disparate technologies and perspectives, must therefore be done virtually. "Distributed teams are the only way we can meet these challenges," confirms technology guru Dion Eusepi.

Building Virtual Communities

Peter Bartlett and Dion Eusepi are intimately involved in assisting people who are working on many of these teams. Peter laughs when he is asked what his title is. "I don't know," he replies, referring both to the fact that titles change rapidly inside of the company and to the fact that nobody really cares what your title is at HP. He has to take out his card and look at it. "It says here that I'm a program manager," he says. Program Managers at HP are senior-level leaders or experts who work on high-priority projects. "I guess I see myself as the chief community architect at HP," he says. Bartlett helps people who don't work within shouting distance of each other feel like they are part of a community, not just cogs in the machinery required to put out products. When done well, this creates a sense of belonging and also improves commitment, productivity, and quality.

Adds Eusepi, "I think of Peter as a community organizer, and me as the process technology manager for virtual communities (like product development teams)." That isn't what his card says, either.

Due to the highly sensitive nature of their work, Bartlett and Eusepi are not able to share specific examples of products or services under development at HP. But they have a great deal to share about the common challenges associated with distance product development.

Keeping Projects on Track

Perhaps the central concern of the distance product development manager is keeping projects on schedule. In HP being on time is often even more important than being within budget. Lost market share due to a late introduction can wash out the entire profit stream of a product now that high-tech products become obsolete so quickly. So how do they manage extremely tight schedules with a distributed team? The key is having good information.

Information about critical path items, progress updates, schedule snags, and so forth are the things that enable leaders to avert disaster and coordinate complicated interrelated activities. This is difficult by itself. But to further complicate matters, these leaders are normally multiplexed on several projects at the same time. In other words, they may be the project leader for one project and an individual contributor on a few others simultaneously.

Information Without Overload

"One of the biggest challenges program and project managers face at HP is how to stay informed about project status without becoming buried with too much information," says Eusepi. A related challenge is to find ways to share this information with others on the product development team in a way that is tailored to their specific needs. What can they do to stay up to date on their various projects?

There are two categories of answers to this question. The first category is the technical system—the technologies that aid the distance leader to track project progress and share important information with the team. The second category has to do with the social system—the people interactions that are required to keep things going at maximum velocity. We will discuss both.

The Technical Solution

Let's start with an illustrative technology. We'll look at how one part of HP has created an information technology aid to assist distance product development managers. It is a general framework that allows both leaders and team members to keep records of their projects on secure intranet systems. Using this technology allows them to stay connected to each other, and it facilitates and focuses meetings ("Let's all look at this together and see if we can come up with an alternative"). It is a substitute for hierarchy. Anyone can look at the information and see where the potential problems are, and better understand the context surrounding the project. Like any information technology tool, it is only as good as the quality and timeliness of the data entered into it, but early results of the application look very promising.

This application has an important characteristic. It is what Eusepi refers to as *personalization and affiliation*—the ability to adapt the technology to individual needs in much the same way that you can customize the Yahoo! search process into a "my Yahoo!" Web page with the format and content you desire. This requires a different approach than the monolithic "one size fits all" IT approaches that have been common in other corporate situations. If one project team likes to organize its information in a way that is different from how another team wants to organize its information, that is fine—within limits. There are what Eusepi calls *megarules,* the boundary conditions, so to speak, that all project participants must follow so that the information they provide can interface appropriately with the system and with the other project data.

Categorizing Information by Role

Hewlett-Packard has also learned from their experience that how you categorize the project information is critical. This helps filter information overload problems. Their particular solution also helps people to retain a sense of identity—an important consideration in the confusing world of multiplexed product development teams.

"A key," says Eusepi, "is to provide information that is role-specific." If you toggle on the program manager view you get high-level information such as schedule information for multiple projects, financial status of program activities, key technology development updates, and project context information (how one project may affect another). This is what Eusepi calls the "20,000-foot" view. Project manager information comes down a few thousand feet. It accesses data about a specific project, including things like critical time frames and task assignments.

It highlights key dependencies and linkages. The team member view is more task-oriented. It digs deeper (several thousand more feet) into information such as what work has been done and what hasn't, and how your particular assignments fall on the critical path schedule (if X slips it won't put the project behind, but if Y slips it will). Eusepi emphasizes the flexibility of this approach. "If a project team uses five roles instead of the normal three roles, the framework can accommodate that."

The project records can be programmed with alerts and triggers to highlight especially important data. These can be set by anyone—not just the distance leader. This fosters the openness and honesty that is an important part of the HP way, and allows the people closest to the action to alert leaders to potential problems quickly. In addition, any person can access any role information regardless of their assignment on the team. With the caveat that proprietary information needs to remain proprietary by the team members, HP wants everyone working on the project to be as fully informed as possible. This includes knowing the bigger picture—what Bartlett calls the *context* of the project: how it fits with other projects, resource constraints and dependencies, the business implications of slipping a schedule, and so forth.

The Social Solution

On the social side, HP has found that there are a number of things the best leaders do to help product development teams be effective. Selecting the right people for the projects, of course, is a key consideration. Ideal team members are not only technically but socially competent. It does little good to have a team member who has world-class knowledge but is either incapable of discussing it with colleagues or unwilling to do so because he or she doesn't understand the importance of collaboration. Knowing what to do with them at project completion is another important consideration—especially if their project ends before another one requiring their services begins (this is seldom a problem at HP).

Things we have discussed in earlier chapters at some length, such as an effective start-up, role clarification activities, and effective ongoing communication practices, are also important and utilized at the company. But Bartlett emphasizes another social solution as well—understanding the different forums for working with people and using them appropriately. We'll discuss this as our concluding solution for distance product development leaders.

Using the Right Interaction Forums

Says Bartlett, "Every forum has its advantages and disadvantages. For example, using a face-to-face meeting to fill out a matrix or do something that could be done virtually is a waste of time." Similarly, other things are better done face-to-face. The best distance product development leaders know when to use what forum and become highly skilled at facilitating them.

Bartlett recommends using virtual interaction in a way that simulates face-to-face meetings. "Face-to-face meetings are more forgiving," he suggests. There is a wider acceptable margin of error when you are physically present with the other members of the team. "Virtual space is not as forgiving." Problems are magnified. It's harder to facilitate a teleconference or videoconference meeting because you don't have everybody in the same room. "But you can do things to simulate many of the face-to-face advantages," he says.

Bartlett gives an example. In a face-to-face meeting with new people in it you have everybody introduce themselves to create that feeling of community. Effective virtual meetings in HP start that way too. But in a virtual meeting you may have to do a little more work than just ask everybody connected by telephone, for example, to say their name and job title. Try to simulate the richness of a face-to-face introduction where people can watch the facial expressions, body language, or physical humor of another person. That takes longer to do virtually than physically. "We sometimes share biographies, stories, use videotape of people introducing themselves, or find ways for people to personalize their virtual workspace with graphics that represent who they are as a person," he reports.

Bartlett reiterates that face-to-face meetings have advantages that can be simulated in a virtual environment with some effort. "If you're at an off-site meeting distributing tasks on a project, you can usually see whether people understand their assignment or not. If it looks like they are confused you take a little extra time to clarify things. But you have to figure out how to do that in a virtual meeting [without video]." You don't have the benefit of looking at body language like the puzzled expression or glazed-over eyes that might indicate confusion.

Bartlett recommends doing things to get people involved—like the polling process we described in earlier chapters. "If you periodically ask people if they understand, or if you regularly ask them questions during the meeting, you are able to test their understanding and modify your meeting accordingly," he notes. "You also get people out of the mode of thinking that a virtual meeting means that you just sit back and listen." He sometimes programs polling questions into his presentations. He might ask everyone to respond periodically to yes/no questions that can quickly be tabulated. "Oops," he might say, "It looks like I lost three of you on that last point. Let me say it differently and see if I can make it more clear."

Simultaneous electronic whiteboard work is also useful. "Working on a whiteboard also helps to simulate a face-to-face environment. It helps you keep a record of the meeting and facilitates polling," he says. When using whiteboards, people can build on one another's points and ask questions. And those who aren't as strong in the language in which the meeting is being conducted as in their own native tongue may be able to express themselves more clearly in a written format than in a verbal one.

Simulating a face-to-face meeting in the several ways Bartlett has reviewed so far can be very useful, but as we mentioned in Chapter 12, "The Necessity of Face-to-Face Meetings," he cautions against the widespread notion that face-to-face meetings are always superior to virtual meetings. "If the meeting is in English and your first language is Japanese or Chinese, you need processing time to think," he notes. An asynchronous forum (e.g., a series of e-mails, etc.) gives you a chance to read the material at your own pace and prepare your English comments. You may have difficulty doing that if you have to respond immediately to someone else in the face-to-face meeting. For this reason, HP actually has seen instances where these virtual forums were more effective at increasing employee involvement than real-time face-to-face meetings were.

Summary

As this HP story illustrates, the answer to the question, "How do we lead product development teams from a distance?" has at least two answers. One answer is that that effective use of information technology helps the distance manager to stay informed, to inform others, and to filter information overload. Doing this well, of course, is a considerable challenge. But having a flexible and customizable system helps—especially if it can be focused on roles rather than on activities. The second answer to the question is to make the best possible use of the people, which, according to Eusepi and Bartlett, is even more difficult than mastering the technology. But selecting appropriate forums for interactions and working to simulate face-to-face activities in a virtual meeting are useful.

The Distance Senior Manager at Weyerhaeuser

Bill (the distance executive) and Jerry (the on-site leader) made a good team—one was a visionary executive and the other a pragmatic operations leader.

Jay Mehta, Vice President of Strategic Marketing
Weyerhaeuser Wood Products

BILL BLANKENSHIP IS an experienced executive with Weyerhaeuser, the forest products giant headquartered in Federal Way, Washington. He presides over three businesses with 2300 employees scattered across 15 locations from Oregon to Pennsylvania. He is connected virtually to his businesses through a variety of communication technologies and holds regular videoconferences with representatives from the various units. Like other distance executives, he regularly faces the normal challenges associated with leading from afar.

But nowhere were the risks or the opportunities of managing from a distance more critical than when a significant business turndown affected one of his largest businesses. In this chapter we will consider this turnaround story as a window to the work of distance executives and review the key leverage activities available to them. With essential help from his on-site partner Jerry Mannigel, Blankenship was able to overcome many of the challenges associated with living at a distance from the operation he oversaw as an executive. In particular, we will see how Blankenship supported something that served as a virtual executive—an on-site aid to decision making on the intranet—which provided a substitute for his regular physical presence at a remote site.

Background

The business that needed to be turned around is located in Marshfield, Wisconsin—some distance from the Weyerhaeuser headquarters location in Washington where Blankenship works. The Midwestern site is home to two businesses: (1) architectural doors, custom wood veneer doors built to architect's specifications, and related components; and (2) specialty door products such as particleboard door cores, created through the "steam thru" manufacturing process. The architectural door business was the one with the problems.

In the fall of 1993 about 600 employees worked on-site at Marshfield in the architectural door business (the 12 salespeople worked out of their homes located around the country). The plant ran multiple shifts in a facility spread over 28 acres. The United Brotherhood of Carpenters and Joiners represented the hourly work force. "The plant had a good work ethic," says Blankenship. "Because of the strong German and Scandinavian cultures in Wisconsin and Iowa, most door and window plants have been located there to benefit from the traditional craftsmanship and pride of the workers."

The site had been started up in the 1890s and was acquired by Weyerhaeuser in 1961 from another corporation. For several years after the acquisition it had been quite successful. Business was strong, and the company was reaping profits without major investments. Then, from 1976 to 1988, the market demand almost doubled as production went from 2.6 to 4.4 million doors. The business rode the wave of success.

The door plant enjoyed a 12-week order file and made 3 to 4 million pre-tax dollars a year. It was producing 8500 to 9500 doors a week.

The strong market and accelerated depreciation laws for office buildings encouraged even more building. Competitors rushed in during 1980–1988 to take advantage of the market. But the bottom fell out just as suddenly as the boom began when demand dropped to 1976 levels in the early 1990s.

The plant experienced serious financial problems. Even though the company was making the same number of doors as before, it began losing money. Management had to take action. They reorganized by business lines during a major refocusing effort supported by a large external consulting firm. Per the firm's recommendation, the company went outside of Weyerhaeuser and hired a new door manager in 1990. Although some measures improved, other things didn't. It wasn't enough. The door business needed a fairly quick but sustainable turnaround. Without dramatic improvement, Blankenship feared that he would be forced to shut down the facility.

The Turnaround

As any good distance executive would, Blankenship first tried to minimize the problems associated with leading the turnaround from afar. He realized that on-site management was crucial. Confirms Bill Barhydt, the CEO of WebSentric, "The on-site leadership is critical for the effective operation of a company. If you want to be successful as a senior executive, make sure you have really good executives in place on location."

Blankenship recruited Jerry Mannigel as the new on-site vice president of operations, reporting directly to him. Jerry had been running the adjoining door core plant successfully. He had started his career as a production employee in the door operation and had special credibility with the workforce.

To make this turnaround project a priority, Blankenship also decided to leverage the most precious resource a distance executive has: He would spend a significant amount of his time in Wisconsin until the business turned the corner. With these two interventions he created an important bridge over the distance, time, and culture gaps between headquarters and the door production site.

But Blankenship knew that even these efforts wouldn't be enough. He was convinced that the turnaround would require changes from every employee in the large operation. They would each need to know what the changes were, and why those changes were necessary, and they would need to be able to execute the changes as well. The logistics of that kind of an effort for such a large facility with so many employees were difficult at best.

Blankenship's personal face-time with employees would be minimal, not only because of limits on when he could be on-site, but because of these logistics. Why was that important? He and Mannigel were convinced that they would need to do something that would engage the entire workforce without requiring constant executive oversight—and they would need to do it quickly. How could they mobilize a rapid and effective response that would change the jobs, thinking, and technologies of all 600 employees distributed over time, space, and culture?

They decided that they would need some sort of single-minded focus that would serve as a type of virtual executive. It would need to be a powerful and constant reminder of business needs whether or not the human executives were present—an infrastructure that would be an ongoing impetus for realigning the work and refocusing the business processes to get continuously improving results. Not only would this help address the problems of distance leadership, but it would also help the employees generate a higher level of commitment to the change. When employees felt they were doing what was required by the business and by customers, rather than feeling like they were merely implementing the wishes of remote senior management, Blankenship and Mannigel felt sure that the turnaround would be more successful.

Before they decided on the virtual executive process they would need more data. The two VPs decided the best thing to do was a walk-through of the plant to assess the situation firsthand. They found out that the managers and systems focused on making "perfect" custom doors to any specifications—that was the basis of the plant's well-known lifetime warranty. Although that sounded good at first blush, Blankenship recalls being strongly concerned that this wasn't the right strategy for the business. "I think we need to decide what our most important strategic initiatives are," he remembers thinking.

They also discovered a disturbing amount of old inventory. Part of the plant had four floors. The bottom floor was used to store 12,000 to 15,000 surplus doors. There were also lots of old dusty doors by the workstations. Some people were identified as expediters to speed doors through the factory. Two full-time people were "door finders," whose job was to find "lost" doors—doors whose exact location in the manufacturing process was unknown. This was frequently necessary to identify and then expedite special "hot" orders, a not-infrequent process of moving certain doors ahead in the queue to placate eager customers. The lead-time for getting a premachined, factory-finished door once the order got to the plant was 6 to 8 weeks, including 3 to 4 weeks to get the order from the salespeople into the work order system and out onto the floor. The work orders were rehandled about eight times (the salespeople took the order on paper; it was later put into the computer; then a paper ticket was created to follow the door around; etc.). Each of these rehandlings was an opportunity to introduce more errors, as evidenced by the slightly off-spec inventory cluttering the factory.

The Slammer Lab

In an especially telling interview at the slammer test lab, Blankenship and Mannigel asked people why they were slamming the doors. Engineers proudly responded that their doors would survive 1 million slams and that they had a goal of increasing that to 2 million. They were actively seeking advanced structural designs, new adhesives, and other materials to meet the goal. Blankenship was puzzled. "What is industry standard?" he asked. "250,000 slams," was the reply. "I never saw these kinds of architecturally designed doors slam at all," Blankenship recalled. "They all had closures like spring-loaded hinges on them to prevent slamming." Was door-slamming the right quality measurement? What were other key measures and what behavior were they encouraging?

The problems were slowly becoming clear to Blankenship and Mannigel. Perhaps the best thing Blankenship could do for the business as a distance executive was help the operation get clear on its strategies and then help put together systems and processes consistent with that strategic direction. Then this system could act like the virtual executive that would motivate and inform employees, whether he or Mannigel was present or not.

They put together a turnaround plan. The roadmap for the turnaround was called the "Starburst Chart" (see Figure 24.1). It was shared with every employee in the plant in a series of meetings that will be discussed after we review value propositions.

Value Propositions and Delivery Systems

According to Jay Mehta, the Weyerhaeuser vice president of strategic marketing for wood products, who served as the internal consultant to the turnaround, a *value proposition* is a way of clearly identifying the core purpose of the organization as perceived by the customers. Once this purpose is identified, it is written in simple language that is measurable. It is then used to evaluate the effectiveness of current processes and systems. Things that don't fit the new value proposition must be eliminated or modified.

Using a diagonal slice (representatives from a variety of levels and jobs), Mehta and the team interviewed customers to identify their needs, create the proposition, and contrast it to current practices. This involvement would create more employee ownership of the virtual executive process than if Blankenship were to develop the proposition by himself and then ask remote employees to implement it. It would also be driven by data rather than by executive preference. Moreover,

Figure 24.1   The Starburst Chart

once the employees understood how to develop the proposition, they would be better able to respond without waiting for executive intervention when customers required changes.

The cross section of people decided that if the plant had had a clear value proposition in the past, it probably would have been, "We manufacture the most durable doors with the most features and options available at competitive prices." After all, every door was engineered to order and assembled to order, with about 3.5 million possible door combinations. "But when we talked to customers," Blankenship recalls, "what they most wanted was uniform and consistent appearance, doors which fit the opening, and door delivery complete and on time."

Doors, the value proposition team discovered, are often the last part of a large construction project. If the customers don't get their doors finished to specification and delivered to the construction site on time, the entire project may be delayed. To deal with this endemic problem, customers had to put on substitute doors until the right ones arrived a few days or weeks later. This was an enormously costly and frustrating process, and nobody in the industry was meeting this vital customer need.

The team discovered that on average only 60 percent of the doors manufactured at the Marshfield plant were complete and on time. Lots of the doors delivered were either too wide or too narrow by $\frac{1}{16}$ of an inch or more, which is enough to trash the door. The devil is in the detail. "You can't shim architectural doors," emphasizes Blankenship. "They must fit the door openings precisely or they're garbage."

Moreover, they discovered that although most doors were "built to grade" (met specification), they were not necessarily consistent with the other doors that would be placed in the same building. In other words, although each door would look fine alone, the group of doors would not necessarily look like they belonged together (with similar grain patterns, color matched for the order, etc.).

Of course, the customers appreciated having millions of possible customized doors available to them. But what they wanted even more than that, *and what they were willing to pay a premium price for,* wasn't the nearly unlimited door options. Rather, it was getting the doors delivered faster, to the agreed specifications, and having them match each other. This is what Mehta calls "the experience valued by the customer"—the thing that must be determined to create an effective value proposition.

A Service-Focused Value Proposition

The value proposition team found that they had to shift from a proposition focused on product to a proposition focused on service. After a great deal of research, debate, and involvement by employees, leaders, and customers, they settled on a new value proposition. It took seven months to complete the process. "We argued about the value proposition for some time," says Blankenship. "It's easy to write a statement without facts and data, but that's not worth a d———. You work up to the summary statement *after* the work (customer interviews, employee discussions, etc.) is done, not *before.*"

The proposition they agreed to, notes Blankenship, is the one listed in Figure 24.2 under the heading "New Value Proposition." "What we were willing to bet our business on," he adds, "was that if we can deliver superior value 100 percent of the time we will get more volume, higher margin, industry consolidation, price improvements, and ultimately superior shareholder value." He turned out to be right.

But making the shift wasn't easy. Although the new proposition may not appear to the casual observer to be dramatically different, Blankenship and Mehta confirm that is was a huge cultural departure from the past. Goals, measures, reward systems, information technology, jobs, communication methods, and a myriad of other value proposition delivery systems would have to be changed.

Old Value Proposition	*New Value Proposition*
"We manufacture the most durable doors with the most features and options available at competitive prices."	"We supply doors and accessories that are: • Uniform and consistent in appearance • Hassle-free • Deliver on specified dates and times (and faster) • For a premium price."

Figure 24.2   Value Proposition Comparison

Communication Processes

"People didn't know how bad shape the business was in," comments Blankenship. To help them understand and discuss the value proposition idea, Bill and Jerry instituted a quarterly review meeting for all employees. This necessitated essentially shutting down the plant once a quarter. They held 13 meetings to get through all shift crews. Eventually they got it down to 3 meetings, getting together in the Knights of Columbus hall in town. "The first two quarter meetings were nasty," recalls Blankenship of verbal rock throwing by disgruntled employees. But the meetings paid off as employees came to see the business facts and data firsthand from their management and union leaders, who cohosted the sessions. In the third quarter all the rocks went away.

For five years, the Starburst Chart was discussed at every quarterly meeting. To make it interesting and memorable, videos and banners were used. The new value proposition became known as "the new train in town." "Some people couldn't get on the train," reiterates Blankenship. "Those who could only pay lip service had to leave." According to the distance executive, "It took two to three years before people believed we were going to stay the course. When employees believed, then customers believed."

Other communication processes were initiated as well. Closed-circuit TV was put in the break rooms to provide a variety of real-time communications composed of video stills with captions but no sound. "WMTV" (Weyerhaeuser Marshfield Television) hired an ESPN network cameraman to provide an ongoing feed of news, weather, and company information, and to film internal interviews with his Sony low-light betacam. It is now the only plant-approved screen saver.

Still other information-sharing forums were established as well. Weekly information meetings with supervisors were started, and each production team had at least a 30-minute mandatory shift meeting every week, too.

Blankenship reminds us, however, that communication is about much more than meetings and technology. It's ultimately about a relationship—a type of personal connection with people. "When I was in town I sometimes spent eight hours straight just walking the plant floor and talking with people," he recalls. Obviously he couldn't talk to all 600 people personally on a regular basis. No distance manager could.

But he thought it was very important to be seen as available and approachable. "People believe you when you're giving them the same message individually you gave them in groups. They knew I was commuting away from home and my family. They knew I cared about them to make those kinds of sacrifices. They knew they could talk to me directly about problems. I made the time to watch them work. Improving a business is about improving relationships."

Roles, Responsibilities, and Relationships

The new value proposition would require new roles and responsibilities in addition to new relationships. Expeditors, for example, would have to be shifted into different value-adding roles as the systems that currently required them were improved. Leadership would have to walk the talk around the proposition.

Blankenship knew, for example, that as a distance executive he would need to stay the course when it got tough. It did and he did. Not even salespeople were allowed to move doors out of the queue. Some employees had to be replaced for continuing practices that were inconsistent with the new value proposition. One of the new delivery systems required was something they called "oldest order first." In order to fix the order system, shorten lead times, and ensure on-time delivery, the plant instituted a process of running each door through the process from start to finish without losing its place in line. This was a marked departure from the past.

The earlier practice in manufacturing was to run all doors with similar equipment set-ups at the same time. This reduced the need for frequent, time-consuming set-ups, but it meant that some doors might have waited several days longer than other doors that happened to have the same set-up requirements as the doors run previously. Measuring and rewarding throughput speed had caused this practice (numbers of doors to go through a work station per hour). Numbers of doors per hour as a measure was summarily eliminated.

Mannigel and Blankenship informed employees that eliminating this process was key to plant survival, and that people would be warned only once or twice prior to being terminated if a newer door was run before an older door. One supervisor was terminated one week and another was released in another couple of weeks, but it still wasn't working. Blankenship and his team got on airplanes and went to customers to tell them it would get worse before it got better. It eventually did get better as Blankenship and Mannigel refused to buckle to the pressure to revert to the way things were done before.

Information Systems

One of the most important technologies required for consistently delivering the value proposition was a new integrated information system. An enterprise resource planning (ERP) system would be necessary to integrate the customer orders, material procurement, inventory control, accounts payable and receivable, and virtually every other manufacturing, human resource, or finance information system. This was not an easy or inexpensive fix. "The ERP was necessary," Mannigel adds, "not because it was trendy to put in an information system, but because it was essential for us to be able to deliver the value proposition better than anyone else."

The information system they required would initially cost over $10 million—a lot for a medium-sized business, and several times more than could normally be justified through the Weyerhaeuser capital expenditure authorization process. But approval came because the system was integral to meeting the value proposition. It was a risk, both for the business and for Blankenship's and Mannigel's personal careers.

Dubbed "Door Builder"™ by the plant, the ERP was technology at its finest. It was software run over a company intranet to meet the seemingly impossible demands of Blankenship's vision. He insisted on a fully integrated database with one-time data entry (no rehandling of orders) that results in a 50 percent reduction in cycle time from the time the order is placed until it arrives at the customer location.

The resulting information system is very complex; so complex that one of the key system vendors said it was impossible and quit. According to the vendor, the required system was more complicated than the one they had put in place for manufacturing the Boeing 777. Internal company programmers aided by some consultants had to finish the work themselves. At the time of implementation it was one of Oracle's most active databases in the world, with 500 transactions per second.

Why so complex? Even with a streamlined number of door offerings necessitated by the value proposition, there are still millions of variables created by the customized door options. For example, the software takes over 25,000 rules into consideration as door orders are entered, to check buildability, fire codes per location, order cost, materials availability, and so forth. If the order is approved for building, order cost is determined. If the customer authorizes the cost, it goes straight to scheduling (bypassing sales) and is scanned at workstations along the way for tracking purposes. The data is never rehandled.

The orders can be placed directly by customers through a company extranet. At the time of this writing, 40 to 50 percent of door orders are received directly from customers and what Blankenship refers to as "territory pirates"—customers who buy and sell extra doors to other customers who can still get them faster from these resellers than from other Weyerhaeuser competitors.

The process was not without complications. An external programmer accidentally deleted the database once when the last backup was two and a half days old. They had problems off and on for nearly a year. It is also too big for a viable Web-based application but will be available as soon as Web bandwidth (and customer technical capacity) increases.

Results

The results of the distance turnaround at Weyerhaeuser's Marshfield door plant are remarkable. Let's consider just a few statistics:

1. Safety improved dramatically. Accidents decreased from a normal weekly activity to a rare occurrence.
2. In an industry where the average lead time is still 8 to 12 weeks, the customers who send orders to salespeople are now getting their custom Weyerhaeuser doors in 6 to 8 weeks. Those who enter their orders directly on the extranet get doors in 2 to 4 weeks. This is any door anytime. The process of expedited doors has been discontinued.
3. The enterprise resource planning (ERP) return on investment is more than 40 percent.
4. The number of management levels has been reduced from five to three.

5. The percentage of doors on time and complete has increased from a low of 40 percent to 99+ percent consistently by 1999. Reminds Blankenship, "It got worse before it got better."
6. Market share increased from 12 percent to the mid-20s in a flat market.
7. The business grew from 600 to 900 employees.
8. Production increased from 400,000 doors to 800,000 doors per year.
9. Pretax earnings reached all-time highs. They even exceeded the peak years of the early 1980s. Cash flow increased fourfold over the same period.
10. Return on net assets (RONA) increased to double digits.

Most important, a business was saved. "People stop me now to thank me," notes Blankenship. Confirms Mehta, "Bill and Jerry saved the business. They are saviors to this plant."

"We are now delivering the value proposition," adds Blankenship. "We are not the low-cost supplier. In some cases we may be the mid or high bidder, but we still get the job and are the preferred supplier. We have nearly half of the school market in North America even though in some cases our bid may be higher. Why? Because the contractor will accept a higher price because we deliver the value proposition they want." When asked if he is concerned about sharing this story in a public forum where his competitors might read it, Blankenship replies: "We now have a fundamental competitive advantage. We leaped four years ahead of where we were. We now have the superior value chain."

Keys to Success

What were the keys to success? "The value proposition is the driver," says Blankenship. "If that is not clear the rest doesn't matter. Why have measures without purpose? Process reliability is an example. We did door slams because of the old unspoken value proposition. In the new one it doesn't make any sense. You need to know what your purpose is. For example, we aren't lowering cost, we are improving margin. If you are clear on things like that you understand that sometimes it makes sense, for example, to slow down. Remember, don't focus on the boss's hot button, focus on the value proposition. You and your career will ultimately be better served."

As Blankenship's story illustrates, it is not just the outcome (the value proposition system that came to serve as a type of virtual executive) but also the way the outcome is achieved that is important. Although Blankenship could have come up with the proposition much more quickly by generating it himself, he believed that employee involvement, customer involvement, and high levels of communication with plant members were important both for the quality of the proposition and for the buy-in necessary for effective implementation.

"Face-to-face communication is critical," says Blankenship. "I'm a big believer in getting the whole system together at some regular times. Three times a year you need to stop the plant and talk to them. If you have continuous operations that can't be stopped, then meet in smaller groups. People need to know what's happening. They need to hear it directly from you as frequently as possible."

In between face-to-face communication, Blankenship stays in touch virtually. For example, he uses PC teleconferencing between his office in Washington and Marshfield. He uses e-mail extensively. Although it helps, Blankenship reminds us that virtual presence is inferior to face-to-face. But you can't lead without being there, virtually or otherwise.

"One of the most important lessons learned is staying the course," adds Mehta. "It was critical that Bill and Jerry have and express their conviction about the value proposition. I can think of fifty times when Bill could have folded under pressure. But he didn't. And that made the difference."

The Marshfield saga continues. "As the story goes on," says Mannigel, "new folklore and examples will continue as they climb the next hill and refine their value proposition in the coming months." Why refine it? Continuous improvement is essential to ongoing effectiveness.

Summary

This case illustrates how a distance senior manager can cross time, space, and culture to make large system improvements. By creating a value proposition system to serve as a virtual executive, Blankenship was able to both create and to sustain fundamental change from a distance.

The power of a clear value proposition—a strategic purposing system that helps people stay on track whether the leader is present or not is illustrated in the turnaround. We have also learned about how the DoorBuilder™ on the Intranet and extranet crossed both the distances between shifts (time) and multiple customer locations (space) and enabled changes that would otherwise have likely demanded the consistent personal presence of a senior executive. Active employee involvement in creating the value proposition enabled a culture that helped people to use the technologies effectively. Communication systems like the quarterly meetings, supervisor and team meetings, and WMTV were keys to effective working relationships.

But perhaps most important, we learned that distance executives must stay the course. As the turbulent environment swirls around the organization like a hurricane, team members benefit from the anchoring stability of effective, *consistent* leadership, even if it comes from afar. That may be the key message of this book. While technologies can often aid the distance manager, there is no electronic or mechanical substitution for a visionary and committed leader.

Index

About the Authors

Kimball Fisher and Mareen Fisher are cofounders of The Fisher Group, Inc. and have worked with many Fortune 100 companies to implement high-performance management systems. They have consulted to clients in North America, Western Europe, Asia, and Africa with companies such as Amoco, Apple Computers, Chevron, Corning, Delphi/Delco, Hewlett-Packard, Monsanto, Motorola, NBC, PepsiCo, Procter & Gamble, The Port of Seattle, Shell, and Weyerhaeuser. The Fishers have trained thousands of managers. They are widely published and are popular speakers on teams, leadership, and organization design. Kimball Fisher is author of *Leading Self-Directed Work Teams* and coauthor of *Tips for Teams*.